D0759667

SELECTS

BY MICHAEL KNISLEY

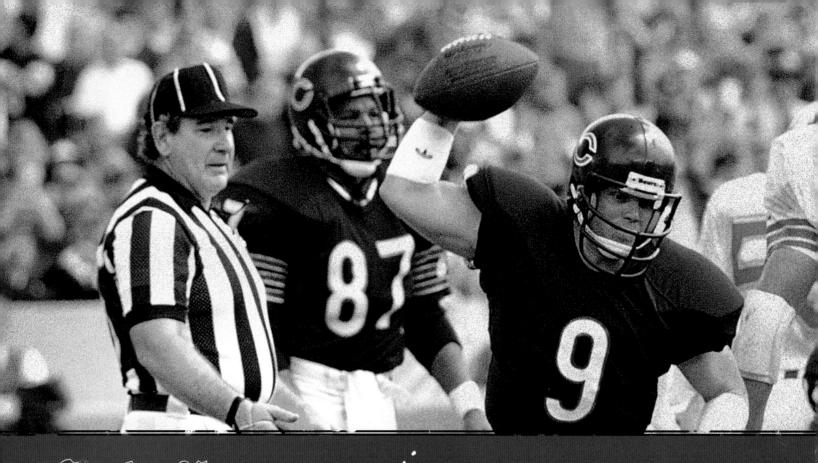

The **SportingNews** SELECTS

Pro Football's

Greatest Teams

CONTENTS

Acknowledgements

The book you see before you is the sixth book of The Sporting News Selects ... series that we have produced. Previously, we selected *Baseball's 100 Greatest Players, Football's 100 Greatest Players, Baseball's 25 Greatest Moments, 50 Greatest Sluggers* and *Stock Car Racing's 50 Greatest Drivers.* By virtue of having gone through the selection and ranking process, you'd think that it would be getting easier.

I can assure you that it's not. Yes, it's fun, but the process of selecting, ranking and then producing all of this in a book is not easy. It takes the work of a committed and talented team —our own "greatest team"—to do this, book in and book out.

So, I must pause to stop, thank and acknowledge a number of people without whom this project wouldn't have gotten done:

—To Michael Knisley, a dedicated friend and longtime colleague whose researching and writing skills were put to the test. Michael has a gift for bringing things to life with his words, a talent he shares with us in this project.

—To Bob Parajon, who coordinated the process of selecting and ranking the teams in this book, in addition to art directing and photo editing.

—To Matt Kindt, who contributed his creative touch in designing this book, and a design and production team led by Dave Brickey and including Steve Romer, Vern Kasal, Pamela Speh, Michael Behrens, Christen Sager and Russ Carr who put a number of finishing touches throughout this book.

—To Ron Smith for editing help.

A common denominator in determining our greatest teams was winning. That's no different than the team we assembled to produce this book.

Steve Meyerhoff
Executive Editor
TSN Books Publishing Group

Copyright © 2002 by The Sporting News, a division of Vulcan Sports Media, 10176 Corporate Square Drive, Suite 200, St. Louis MO 63132. All rights reserved.

No part of Pro Football's Greatest Teams may be reproduced or transmitted in any form or by any means, electronic or mechanical, including photocopy, recording or any other information storage and retrieval system now known or to be invented, without permission in writing from the publisher, except by a reviewer who wishes to quote brief passages in connection with a review written for inclusion in a magazine, newspaper or broadcast.

The Sporting News is a federally registered trademark of Vulcan Sports Media, Inc. Visit our website at www.sportingnews.com. ISBN: 0-89204-693-7

Introduction

Defining "greatness" is a challenging task. Oh, it makes for great conversation: Who's the greatest quarterback of all-time? What's the greatest performance of all-time? Who among us hasn't had that conversation with family and friends.

Well, having a conversation, a debate, an argument, is much easier than committing that opinion on paper and putting it in a book. That's permanence. That's finality. That's the end of debate, so to speak.

When we turned our "selective" attention to the greatest football teams of all-time, we did so with open eyes. We've selected the greatest baseball and football players, we've selected the greatest NASCAR drivers and the greatest baseball moments; we have experience, and we used that experience as we pulled together this book.

As we worked through the process of selecting and ranking the greatest football teams of all-time, we used few criteria to frame the list. We didn't dictate that the greatest teams had to have won a Super Bowl or an NFL championship. We didn't dictate that the greatest teams had to come from the post-AFL/NFL merger. The process began with an open field.

As we culled through the hundreds of teams and seasons, it did become clear that the greatest teams shared a few common attributes. One was dominance, achieved on a game-by-game basis and further reflected by an overwhelming successful win-loss record. A second was a championship. A good team that had a successful regular season but didn't win the season's championship was difficult to call "great." Great teams found a way to overcome obstacles, injuries and losses to win when it counted most.

And, so, what you have here is a product of that process. And though it's in print form, it by no means ends the debate. On the contrary, the debate probably just starts now. We don't expect everyone to agree with everything in our book; you may, in fact, disagree with everything in this book. But then again, there never is unanimity when you try to answer those questions.

As you read this book, you'll see how we rank our greatest teams of all-time. If you want to let us know how you feel about your greatest teams of all-time, drop us an e-mail at editors@sportingnews.com, subject line: NFL's Greatest Teams.

The Teams

1

The 1972 Miami Dolphins could have lost on October 1 in Bloomington, Minn., but they didn't. They beat the Vikings 16-14 with 10 points in the fourth quarter. Bob Griese threw a 3-yard touchdown pass to tight end Jim Mandich with 1:28 to play for the come-from-behind win.

The Dolphins could have lost to Buffalo on October 22 at home in the Orange Bowl, but they didn't. Garo Yepremian kicked a 54-yard field goal, the longest of his career, in the third quarter and Mercury Morris scored on a 15-yard run in the fourth. Miami held off the Bills, 24-23.

They could have lost on November 19 to the Jets, again at home, but they didn't. Somehow, Earl Morrall coaxed a 31-yard touchdown run out of his 38-year-old legs, and Morris scored the winner from 14 yards out as the Dolphins came back from a 17-7 deficit and won 28-24.

They could have lost any of the nine games that Griese, the starting quarterback, missed with a broken right leg and a dislocated ankle. But they didn't. Morrall, a waiver-wire acquisition from the Colts before the season began, was magnificent in his place.

They didn't lose. All the way through 14 regular-season games, two AFC playoff games and Super Bowl VII, the Dolphins didn't lose. Seventeen times, Miami won. That's perfection the NFL hadn't experienced in its first 52 seasons. That's perfection the NFL hasn't experienced in the 30 seasons since 1972.

The Dolphins' offensive line opened gaping holes for Larry Csonka (39), who powered his way to 1,117 yards.

1972 Miami Dolphins

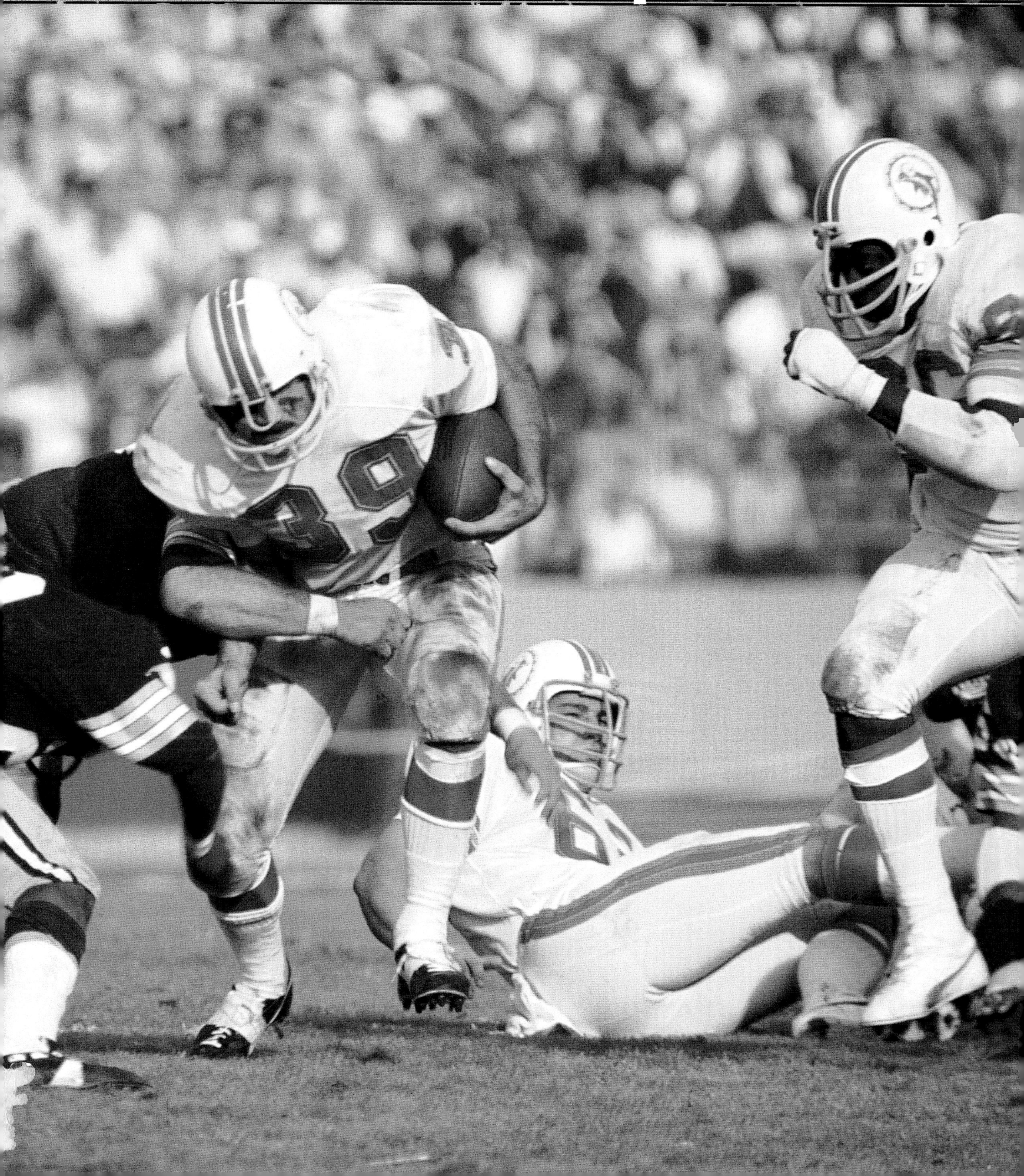

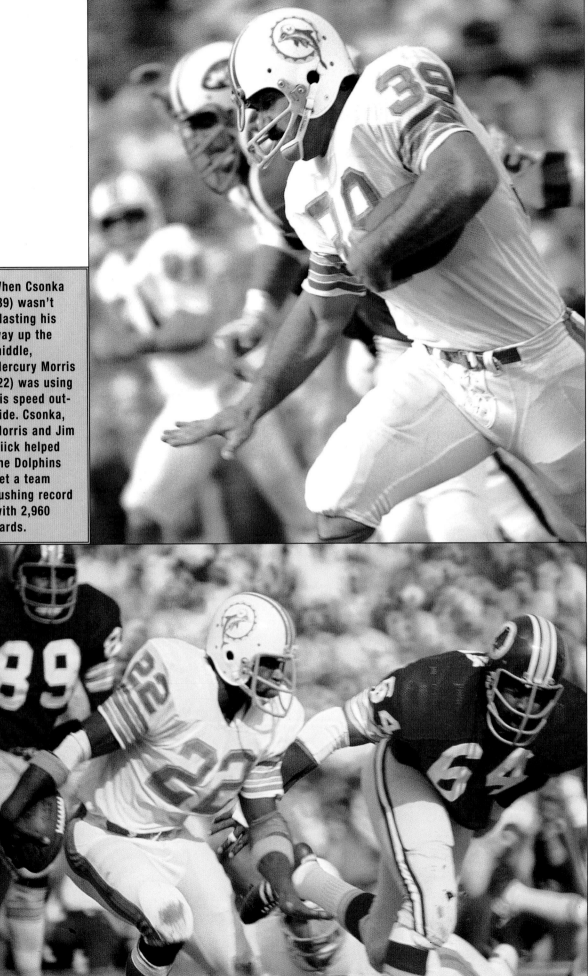

When Csonka (39) wasn't blasting his way up the middle, Mercury Morris (22) was using his speed outside. Csonka, Morris and Jim Kiick helped the Dolphins set a team rushing record with 2,960 yards.

In our book, that makes the 1972 Dolphins the best team in the history of professional football. You can't argue with perfection. Other teams have had overpowering offenses, as the Dolphins did. Other teams have had dominating defenses, as the Dolphins did. Other teams have had extraordinary seasons, as the Dolphins did. But when all of those other teams could have lost, they did. At least once.

No other NFL team has made it through a complete season, including playoffs, without a loss or a tie. End of debate.

In 1972, the Dolphins were the right team with the right coach at the right time to take on all comers and win. Seventeen times.

In the early '70s, professional football was in a ground-game phase, and Miami made the most of the league's heavy emphasis on the run. During the 1971 season, the 26 NFL head coaches called more running plays than they had in any single season since 1960, and fewer passes than in any year since 1959. In 1972, league officials tried to open up the passing game by

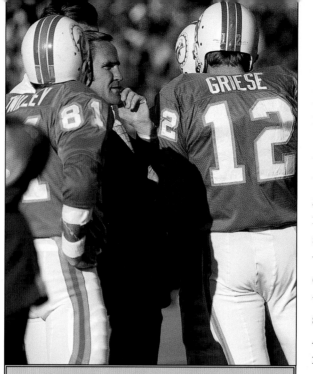

Don Shula had the luxury of two more-than-capable QBs: starter Bob Griese and backup Earl Morrall (below).

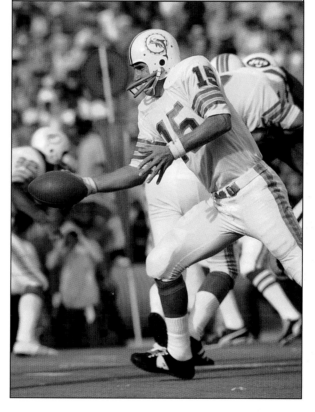

moving the hashmarks closer to the center of the field, the idea being that the change would give receivers more room to roam the short sideline. As it worked out, the change added room to run on the short side of the field, too. A record 10 backs reached the 1,000-yard mark that year.

Nobody ran the ball better than Miami with Morris, Larry Csonka and Jim Kiick. Coach Don Shula and offensive coordinator Monte Clark made run-blocking monsters out of several linemen cast off by other teams, including center Jim Langer (who had been waived by Cleveland), left guard Bob Kuechenberg (who had been released by Philadelphia) and right guard Larry Little (who had been traded by San Diego).

Behind those three and tackles Wayne Moore and Norm Evans, the Dolphins set a team record with 2,960 rushing yards.

Csonka was the power runner for the tough inside yards. Morris was the speedster on the outside. Kiick excelled at catching the ball out of the backfield. Csonka and Morris each gained 1,000 yards or more, the first time an NFL team had two backs reach that milestone in a single season.

Because its running game was so strong, Miami wasn't handicapped as seriously as it might have been by the loss of Griese on a hit by the Chargers' Ron East in the fifth game of the year. The Dolphins didn't need a wide-open passing game to win, so neither Griese nor Morrall threw very often. Against the Bills in one game, they put the ball in the air only 10 times. At the end of the regular season, Miami had called 613 running plays and thrown 259 passes.

The Dolphins' defense gave up passing yardage even more sparingly than their offense gained it. While Griese and Morrall threw for a combined average of 148 yards per game, Miami allowed only 125 passing yards per game.

Together, the offense and defense made for a difficult—no, impossible—combination to beat. The Dolphins scored more points (27.5 per game) and gained more

A strong offensive line gave Griese (below) time to connect with talented receivers like Paul Warfield (above).

yards (359.7 per game) than any team in the NFL, and at the same time gave up fewer points (12.2 per game) and fewer yards (235.5 per game) than any team in the NFL.

The defensive players were neither famous nor flamboyant. In fact, they called themselves the "No-Name Defense" after Dallas coach Tom Landry commented on their lack of notoriety before the Cowboys' 24-3 victory over Miami in Super Bowl VI. But they were simply the best defense in football.

Middle line-backer Nick Buoniconti was its heart and soul, but the defense became known by the uniform number worn by Bob Matheson, a non-starter who was a key to Miami's success against the pass. The "53" defense featured Matheson alternately as a defensive end and a fourth linebacker. From both spots, he started every play standing up, and he could either rush the passer or drop into coverage. That wrinkle gave offenses fits.

In the Super Bowl, Washington double-teamed Buoniconti with blockers. But as a result, the Redskins couldn't handle left tackle Manny Fernandez one-on-one. He finished with 17 tackles. Right end Bill Stanfill and safeties Dick Anderson and Jake Scott, who was named the most valuable player of Super Bowl VII for his two interceptions, were the other high-profile players—that is, if a "No-Name" can have a high profile.

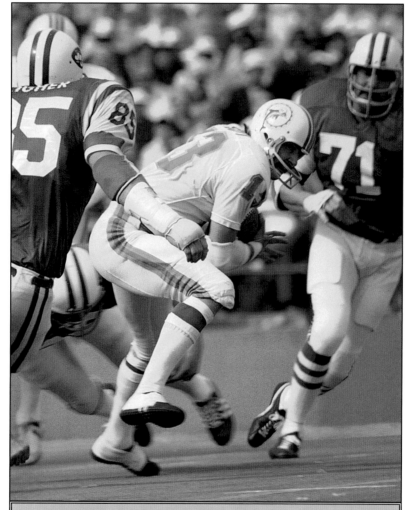

"No-Name" safety Jake Scott (13) earned MVP honors in Super Bowl VII.

Everything fit together. The offense controlled the ball so well that the defense didn't spend an inordinate amount of time on the field. The defense stayed stout enough to keep the offense from needing quick strikes to win shootouts. Shula fostered an all-business atmosphere that kept his team even-keeled, if not exciting to watch. He was the perfect head coach to cope with the growing pressure to stay undefeated.

It didn't hurt that Miami drew one of the easiest schedules in NFL history in 1972. The only other team in the AFC Eastern Division that even reached .500 was the Jets, and their 7-7 record meant the Dolphins clinched the division title on November 19 with a month of the regular season still to play.

Of their opponents, only the Giants (8-6) and the Chiefs (also 8-6) finished with winning records. Combined, the teams the Dolphins played in 1972 were 51-86-2.

Still, Miami beat them all. As often as not, Miami beat them all soundly: 52-0 over New England, 34-13 over Houston, 31-10 over St. Louis, 23-0 over Baltimore.

On November 12 when Miami spanked the Patriots by that 52-0 score, it marked Shula's 100th career victory. In the wake of the victory, he received a congratulatory telegram from then-President Richard Nixon, who had made national news the previous year by suggesting in a late-night phone call to Shula before Super Bowl VI that the Dolphins might have some success against Dallas if they threw to wide receiver Paul Warfield on a down-and-in pattern. The Cowboys, of course, prepared for the play, neutralized Warfield and won.

In his November '72 telegram, Nixon pledged not to call any plays if Miami made that year's Super Bowl. Shula was emphatic with his public thanks. It turned out the Dolphins played the team up the street from the White House in Super Bowl VII, and Nixon went on the record with his support of the Redskins. Shula, no doubt, breathed a sigh of relief.

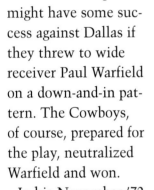

> Together, the offense and defense made for a difficult — no, impossible — combination to beat.

Though remembered for a classic Super Bowl miscue, Garo Yepremian was ever reliable during the Dolphins' perfect season.

When the playoffs began, Morrall was still starting at quarterback. Miami met Cleveland, which had been 10-4 in the regular season. The Browns easily were the best team the Dolphins had faced, and led 14-13 in the fourth quarter. Again, Miami could have lost, but didn't. Late in the game, a pass-interference penalty gave the Dolphins the ball on the 8-yard line, and Kiick scored the winning touchdown from there.

In the AFC Championship Game, Miami and the Steelers were locked in a 7-7 struggle at halftime. The Dolphins could have lost then, too. But Shula realized that Griese was better-equipped than Morrall to handle Pittsburgh's pass rush because he released the ball more quickly. In the third quarter, Shula gambled on bringing Griese off the bench for his first action in nine weeks and Griese took the team on two second-half scoring drives, sparking Miami's 21-17 win.

For most of Super Bowl VII, it appeared the Dolphins couldn't lose. They dominated the Redskins on both sides of the line of scrimmage and led 14-0 late in the game. Through the first two quarters, Washington didn't even

Tacke Manny Fernandez (75) was a key figure in the
"No-Name Defense" that shut down opponents
throughout a perfect 1972 season.

cross midfield. Only one of the most ludicrous plays in Super Bowl history gave the Redskins a chance.

With just over two minutes to play, Washington's Bill Brundige blocked a 42-yard Yepremian field-goal attempt, and Yepremian picked up the loose ball. Rather than protect it, though, the kicker tried to throw a pass. When the ball slipped out of his hand, he batted it into the air, allowing the Redskins'

Mike Bass to snag it and score on a 49-yard return.

Suddenly, the score was 14-7 and Washington had the ball back with 1:14 to play. The Dolphins could have lost, or at least been forced into overtime.

They didn't, and they weren't. On fourth down from the 26-yard line, they sacked Redskins' quarterback Billy Kilmer.

The perfection was complete.

Backup quarterback Earl Morrall (below) won the nine games he started after Griese broke his leg.

The no-nonsense, charge-ahead style of the Dolphins' offense was most evident in two dominating workhorses who would become Hall of Famers: guard Larry Little (66) and fullback Csonka (39), who is sitting next to Kiick.

2

Here's Jerry Kramer, a 6-foot-3, 245-pound pile-driver of a pulling guard on the run around the end. Here's Fuzzy Thurston, 6-1, 247, trailing Kramer from the other guard spot. They have malice on their minds, and it's directed at defensive ends, linebackers, cornerbacks, safeties.

Here's Ron Kramer, the 6-3, 250-pound tight end, bigger even than Thurston and Kramer, blocking down on the inside, flattening the middle linebacker who is in pursuit of the play.

Here's Jim Taylor behind them all at full gallop, the football tucked under an arm, and he isn't just looking for open field. He's looking to punish somebody, too. Yardage is the first objective. But it's better if he can run somebody over as he gains it.

Football has rarely produced a more imposing sight than the Packer sweep. And the Packer sweep was never more imposing than in 1962. Green Bay rolled to a 13-1 record in the regular season and a 16-7 victory over the Giants in the championship game. The Packers did it with the power personified by those offensive linemen, and with the chops-mashing bull-rushes of Taylor, Tom Moore, Paul Hornung, Earl Gros and Elijah Pitts.

Vince Lombardi won five NFL championships in Green Bay, including the first two Super Bowls. But none of his other title teams dominated the league the way his '62 juggernaut did.

The Packers scored 415 points and allowed only 148.

The Packer sweep: Green Bay's offensive line formed a formidable wall for Jim Taylor (31), who punished would-be tacklers.

1962 Green Bay Packers

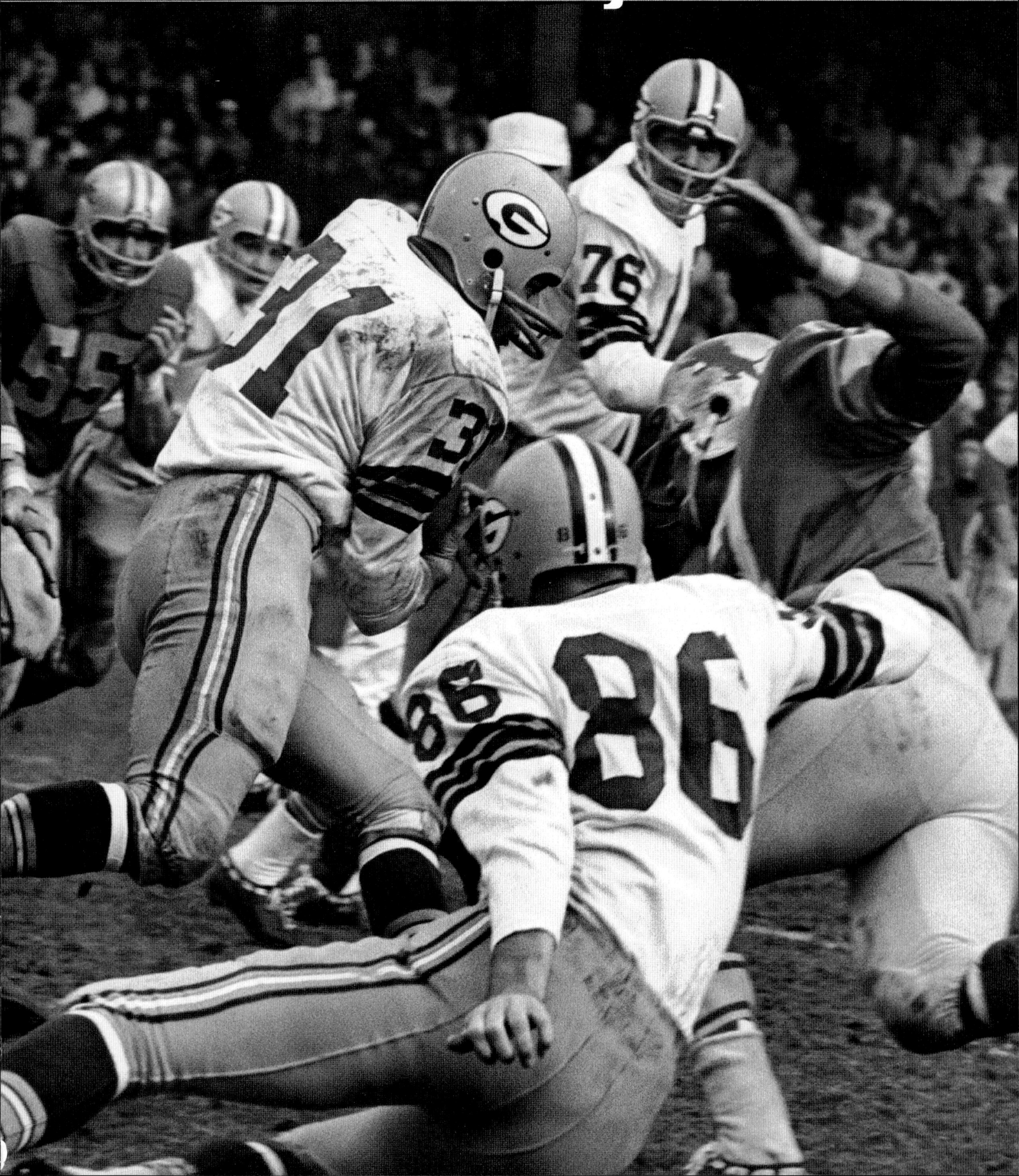

When they weren't overwhelming defenses with the famed Packer sweep and Bart Starr's efficient passing, they were bullying opposing offenses with one of the most talented and intimidating group of tacklers the game has known. At the end of the NFL Championship Game in Yankee Stadium, the most valuable player wasn't Taylor or Starr. It was middle linebacker Ray Nitschke.

All told, 10 players, plus Lombardi, from the 1962 Packers have been inducted into the Pro Football Hall of Fame. Little wonder they muscled their way to the title.

The 1962 season was Lombardi's fourth in Green Bay. In 1958, under Ray "Scooter" McLean, the Packers were 1-10-1. Lombardi coached them to a 7-5 record in his first year and had them in the championship game (where they lost to the Eagles 17-13) by the end of his second season. In 1961, they won it all with an 11-3 regular-season record and a 37-0 shutout of the Giants for the title.

That rapid turnaround didn't come through wholesale roster changes. In fact, 14 of the starters in the championship season of 1961 had been on the 1-10-1 team three years earlier. Instead, over those first three seasons the

Packers had learned, and lived, Lombardi's approach to the game—an approach that emphasized—that demanded—character, backbone and commitment.

By 1962, Lombardi had his team's character, backbone and commitment where he wanted them. Most of those Hall of Fame Packers were in their prime, and they bullied their way through the league like men among boys.

Ten weeks into the season, Green Bay was undefeated. And the Packers, who had also won all six of their exhibition games, had been seriously challenged only twice.

Against Detroit in the fourth game, Green Bay trailed 7-6 in the closing minutes and the Lions had the ball. But instead of running out the clock, Milt Plum, the Lions quarterback, threw a pass intended for receiver Terry Barr. As Barr slipped, Herb Adderley intercepted and Hornung kicked a game-winning field goal. Packers 9, Detroit 7.

The Lions were so incensed about the play that defensive tackle Alex Karras threw his helmet at Plum in the locker room. Joe Schmidt, the team captain, reportedly had to be kept from throwing a punch at his

Behind the great teams, there always is a mastermind. There may have been none greater than Vince Lombardi.

own quarterback, an allegation Schmidt later denied.

The Packers' other close call came in the 10th week, a 17-13 victory over Baltimore. Adderley helped save the day in that game, too, with a 103-yard kickoff return for a touchdown.

Then, on Thanksgiving Day in the 11th game, Green Bay played Detroit again, this time at Tiger Stadium. The Lions, ripe for revenge, came after Starr with a merciless pass rush. Karras and his fellow tackle, Roger Brown,

> Over the first three seasons the Packers had learned, and lived, Lombardi's approach to the game.

inflicted most of the damage. When it ended, Starr had been sacked 11 times, resulting in 110 yards in losses, one safety and one fumble.

The Packers suffered their only loss of the season, 26-14. They finished with easy wins over Los Angeles and San Francisco, and a narrower 20-17 victory in a rematch with the Rams in the regular-season finale.

Taylor, a fullback who ran with defiance, blasted to the NFL rushing crown with 1,474 yards on 272 carries, an average gain of 5.4 yards. His 19 touchdowns also topped the

Although injured much of the year, Paul Hornung (5) played a key role for the Packers—running and kicking.

league. It was his best season, perhaps because the Packers relied on him more than ever as injuries limited Hornung to 57 carries and 219 yards. The 1962 season marked the only year during the great Jim Brown's career that somebody other than Cleveland's fullback led the league in rushing.

Starr, too, had one of his best seasons. His 2,438 passing yards were the most in his 16-year career, and his 62.5-percent completion rate led the league. Ends Max McGee and Boyd Dowler each caught 49 passes. Tight end Kramer grabbed 37 and scored seven touchdowns.

The forward pass was more than an afterthought in Lombardi's offense. But it ran a distant second to the running game, and especially to the Packer sweep. In an era when quarterbacks such as the Colts' Johnny Unitas, the Steelers' Bobby Layne, the Eagles' Sonny Jurgensen and the Lions' Plum were dominating games as never before, Lombardi turned back the game's clock with Green Bay's power rushing attack.

The sweep certainly wasn't new to football.

The offense featured receiver Boyd Dowler (above), but passing played second fiddle to the running game. Jim Taylor (31 below) beat Jim Brown for the rushing crown—the only time in Brown's career someone else won the title.

Running the Packers' multi-faceted attack was quarterback Bart Starr, who enjoyed one of his best seasons.

It had its origins in the single-wing alignment of the 1920s and '30s, which featured linemen leading running backs through holes off the tackles and around the ends. The Packers ran out of a "T" formation, but the basics were the same. In 1962, Lombardi's philosophy was a throwback, and defenses built to counter the pass had great difficulty stopping it.

Then there was the Packers' defense: Willie Davis and Henry Jordan on the line, Nitschke at middle linebacker, Willie Wood and Adderley in the secondary. Those five, all future Hall of Famers, led the way. Nitschke, one of the game's hardest hitters, terrorized every team he faced. Wood led the league in interceptions with nine in 1962. Adderley was a ball-hawk with phenomenal speed.

Through Green Bay's first three games, the defense allowed a total of seven points. The Packers shut out the St. Louis Cardinals, 17-0, in their second game, and blanked the Bears, 49-0, the next week. At the end of the year, the defense led the league in 12 statistical categories. They did it with a fundamental 4-3 alignment and man-to-man coverage. But coordinator Phil Bengston tinkered with the formation by bringing his defensive tackles a little closer into the center of the line to keep the offense's interior blockers occupied. That freed Nitschke to pursue the play.

Which is exactly what he did against the Giants in the championship game on December 30. The weather was bitter. The temperature was

Willie Wood (above), Henry Jordan (74 below) and Willie Davis (87) contributed to a dominant defensive unit.

20 degrees, but the wind blew in 40-mph gusts.

The day was made for defense. The day was made for middle linebackers. The day was made for Nitschke and New York's Sam Huff.

Huff and Taylor went at it all afternoon. Taylor carried the ball 31 times, many of them on the Packer sweep. More often than not, Huff was there to meet him. It became a personal duel, Taylor telling Huff to "hit me harder" as they untangled after another tackle. Taylor never worked harder to gain 85 yards. One of those 31 carries was a 7-yard score in the second quarter, Green Bay's only touchdown that day.

Huff was spectacular, but Nitschke was better. On an early Giants drive, he tipped a pass

The day was made for defense. The day was made for middle linebackers. The day was made for Nitschke and New York's Sam Huff.

that became a Packer interception. He recovered two fumbles, one that set up Taylor's touchdown and another that led to a field goal. He helped keep New York's offense scoreless. The Giants' only touchdown came on a blocked punt that Jim Collier recovered in the end zone in the third period.

Three field goals by Jerry Kramer, who took over the kicking duties at midseason after Hornung was injured, made the difference.

The Packers' dynasty under Lombardi was well under way.

By the time it ended after the 1967 season, they had "swept" to three more championships. But they were never better than they were in '62.

Tackle Forrest Gregg was an offensive anchor, masterful at both protecting Starr and run-blocking.

3

T he Pittsburgh Steelers won four Super Bowl championships in the 1970s, which gives them clear ownership of the title "Team of the Decade." So what makes the 1978 Steelers any better than Pittsburgh's Super Bowl champs of 1974, 1975 and 1979?

Here's what: None of the polkas honoring those other teams had the staying power of "The Steeler Polka (1978 version)."

They must have been good.

Here's how the '78 rendition of "The Steeler Polka" ends:

Offense, Offense, take that football whole way up the field!

Offense, Offense, let's score and score and never ever yield!

Franco, Franco, can you believe we have a running game!

The Steelers are so great, and so hard to overrate,

Good things, will come, to those who work and wait.

Charge!

Okay, so nobody said it was Shakespeare. But Pittsburgh is Polka Country, and this one caught on. The ditty had been around since at least 1973 as a Steeler fight song of sorts—that is, if a polka ever passes muster as a fight song—but the lyrics were updated in '78 and became a local hit for a recording artist named Jimmy Psihoulis.

The '78 song managed to work in Terry Bradshaw, Rocky Bleier, Lynn Swann, Roy Gerela and Mean Joe Greene in addition to Franco Harris. It may not be a

Franco Harris (32) and the Steelers won 14 of 16 regular-season games, then outlasted the Cowboys in Super Bowl XIII.

Mean Joe Greene led a defense that allowed the fewest points in the league (12.2 per game).

coincidence that all of those stars except Greene, the defensive end, and Gerela, the place-kicker, played offense, or that the last verse emphasizes the offense. (The only mentions of offense in the 1973 version are a couple of references to Harris' 1972 rookie season.) For the first time during Pittsburgh's decade of dominance, the 1978 Steelers put an explosive offense on the field to go with their "Steel Curtain" defense.

That, of course, explains why they rate higher than Pittsburgh's other championship clubs. The '78 offense really did "take that football whole way up the field." And quite often, the Steelers did it with a new and exciting tool, at least for a Chuck Noll-coached team: the forward pass.

Bradshaw and his fleet wide receivers, Swann and John Stallworth, played on Pittsburgh's Super Bowl championship teams in 1974 and '75. But those two titles came on the shoulders of unassailable defense and Franco's bruising runs. In 1974, the ground game accounted for 55 percent of the Steelers' offense. In 1976, when Pittsburgh reached the AFC Championship Game but lost to Oakland, the rush accounted for 64 percent of its total yardage.

By comparison, Bradshaw's 2,915 passing yards and NFL-best 28 touchdowns in 1978 seem positively electrifying. Harris rushed for more than 1,000 yards again (he had 1,082), but the ground game in '78 made up just over 46 percent of the Steelers' total offense. As a team, they gained only 3.6 yards per carry. They moved the ball with the pass.

Pittsburgh was finally playing 20th-century football, and "The Steeler Polka (1978 version)" reflected it.

The new, wide-open attack paid dividends early in the season with a razzle-dazzle play that beat the Browns in overtime in the fourth game. Bradshaw flipped the ball to Bleier on an apparent sweep to the right, which became a reverse to

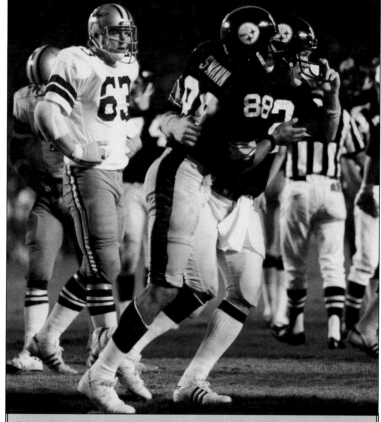

Super Bowl XIII MVP Terry Bradshaw threw four touchdown passes against the Cowboys, including this one to Lynn Swann.

Swann, which became a lateral back to Bradshaw, which finally became a 37-yard touchdown pass to tight end Bennie Cunningham. It's hard to imagine Noll calling that play in such a critical situation three or four years earlier.

Of course, the Steelers didn't forget their roots. The play was set up by a fourth-down Harris plunge that kept the drive alive.

Pittsburgh won its first seven games, with

Bradshaw (right) was one of five offensive starters, and Jack Lambert (below) was one of four on defense who would later be reunited in the NFL's Hall of Fame.

Cleveland providing the only close call. Then in Week Eight, the Steelers got their first look at the new kid on the AFC Central Division block. The Oilers brought Earl Campbell, the No. 1 overall pick in the draft, to town on October 23 for a Monday Night Football date. Campbell was on his way to becoming the first rookie since Jim Brown to win the NFL rushing title, with 1,450 yards. At that point in the season, Pittsburgh was giving up just 106 rushing yards per game, but Campbell gained 89 and Houston had 169 as a team on the ground.

The Oilers put together three long scoring drives and won, 24-17.

The Steelers' only other stumble came on the road, a 10-7 loss to the Los Angeles Rams. The next time they met Houston, on December 3, the "Steel Curtain" smothered Campbell (41 yards) in a 13-3 victory.

In the late '70s, the NFL came out of a long stretch of seasons dominated by run-oriented teams. New rules in 1978 designed to jump-start passing games restricted contact between a defender and a receiver more than five yards downfield, and allowed offensive linemen to pass-block with their arms extended and their hands open. The adjustments worked. Teams began to throw downfield more often and with better results.

So when Noll jazzed up the Steelers' passing game in '78, he was keeping up with, or maybe finally catching up to, the changing times. But he wasn't silly about it. He didn't open up the offense at the expense of his defense. Pittsburgh finished its 14-2 regular season giving up an average of just 260.5 yards per game and allowing the fewest points in the league (12.2 per game). The Steelers' hit-now-and-take-names-later philosophy hadn't changed since their first two Super Bowl victories.

Greene and L.C. Greenwood on the left side

of the line teamed with a rotation of Steve Furness, John Banaszak and Dwight White on the right side to form one of the most effective fronts in football. Noll's 4-3 defensive theory was to have his line jam the offense's big blockers so that Pittsburgh's linebackers were free to make the tackles. In '78, Jack Lambert, Jack Ham and Loren Toews were the beneficiaries of that freedom.

Donnie Shell, one of the game's hardest hitters, played strong safety next to Mike Wagner at free safety. The cornerbacks were Ron Johnson and veteran All-Pro Mel Blount. Some of the longtime members of the "Steel

Pittsburgh defenders Lambert (falling), Loren Toews (51), Dwight White (78) and Joe Greene (75) swarmed opponents.

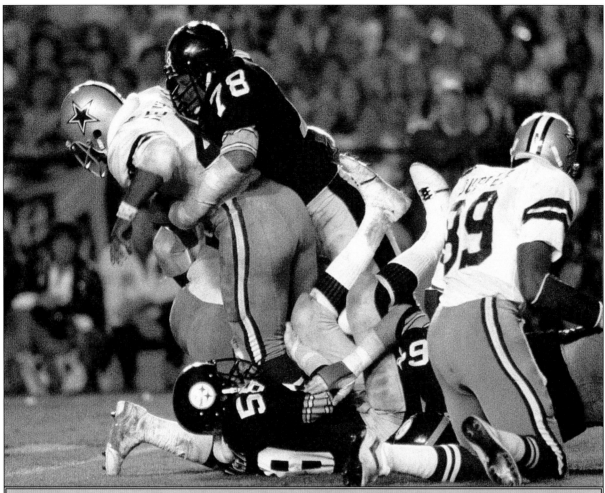

White (78) was a defensive force while Mike Webster (below) manned the center of the offensive line.

Curtain" were nearing the end of their careers, but the defense remained as daunting as it had been in the first half of the decade. The Steelers intercepted 27 passes, recovered 21 fumbles and recorded 44 sacks.

The playoffs began the way the regular season ended—against the defending AFC champion Broncos. Pittsburgh won at Denver, 21-17, to finish the season, and then played host to the Broncos in the divisional playoff round. Swann made a sensational, leaping catch at the goal line for a 38-yard touchdown, and Stallworth caught 10 passes, including a 45-yard TD. Steelers 33, Denver 10.

Then came the third meeting of the year with Campbell and the Oilers, this time in the AFC Championship Game. Played in a freezing rain, the game was a tour de force for

Bradshaw and the "Steel Curtain." The defense intercepted five Dan Pastorini passes and recovered four Houston fumbles.

Three of those fumble recoveries came in a 90-second Oilers' nightmare late in the first half. Pittsburgh was ahead 14-3 when Houston's Ronnie Coleman fumbled with 1:23 to play. Bradshaw threw a 29-yard touchdown pass to Swann. Houston's Johnny Dirden fumbled away the kickoff. Bradshaw threw a 17-yard touchdown pass to Stallworth. On Houston's next play from scrimmage, Coleman fumbled again. Gerela kicked a 37-yard field goal with four seconds left.

The Steelers had scored 17 points in 48 seconds, and put the game away. Campbell finished with only 62 yards on the ground and Pittsburgh won, 34-5.

If there were any remaining doubts about the Steelers' ability to play shoot-out football with a sophisticated passing attack, they vanished in Super Bowl XIII. Bradshaw matched the Cowboys' Roger Staubach pass for pass, completion for completion. Dallas had been playing a high-tech passing game for years; Pittsburgh was new to it. But in the end, Staubach and Bradshaw had nearly identical statistics. They both completed 17 of their 30 attempts, with one interception.

The difference: Bradshaw threw four touchdown passes to Staubach's three, and the Steelers won, 35-31. Staubach almost had a fourth, but Cowboys reserve tight end Jackie Smith dropped a wide-open pass in the end zone in the third quarter. Instead of seven points, Dallas scored three on a Rafael Septien field goal.

When it ended, Pittsburgh had become the first team to win three Super Bowls, lending resonance to another verse of "The Steeler Polka (1978 version)." It goes like this:

We're from the town with that great football team,
We cheer the Pittsburgh Steelers.
Winning's a habit, not only a dream,
Go out and get them Steelers!

By 1978, those Super Bowl wins were becoming a habit, and a hit, in Polka Country.

They were rebels without a pause, these Chicago Bears; and as they bullied their way through the 1985 season, they not only left 18 vanquished foes in their wake, they also ground a series of NFL conventions and rules under their cleats and into the dirt and sod of Soldier Field.

Led by assistant coach Buddy Ryan's innovative "46" defense, the Bears won four games by shutout and held 14 of their 19 opponents to 10 points or less. In their three playoff wins, including Super Bowl XX, they allowed a total of 10 points. They simply brought the rest of the NFL to its knees.

But they were so much more than just one of the best football teams of all time. The Bears of 1985 were the cockiest, most brazen bunch of athletes the world of football has ever seen. They brought charisma and personality to the league, and demanded that a nation of fans pay attention. The nation responded. In the U.S. alone, some 127 million people watched the broadcast of their 46-10 romp over New England in Super Bowl XX, at the time the highest-rated telecast in history. The Bears were a happening, on and off the field.

They were . . . well, different. If there was a football convention to be defied, they defied it. Forget, for instance, the pregame, lip-service praise traditionally given to the opponents. Before Chicago's first playoff game, Ryan predicted a shutout. He got it, 21-0, over

The "46" defense ranked first in the league in points allowed, rushing yards allowed, total yards allowed, first downs allowed, pass-completion percentage, interceptions and turnovers.

1985 Chicago Bears

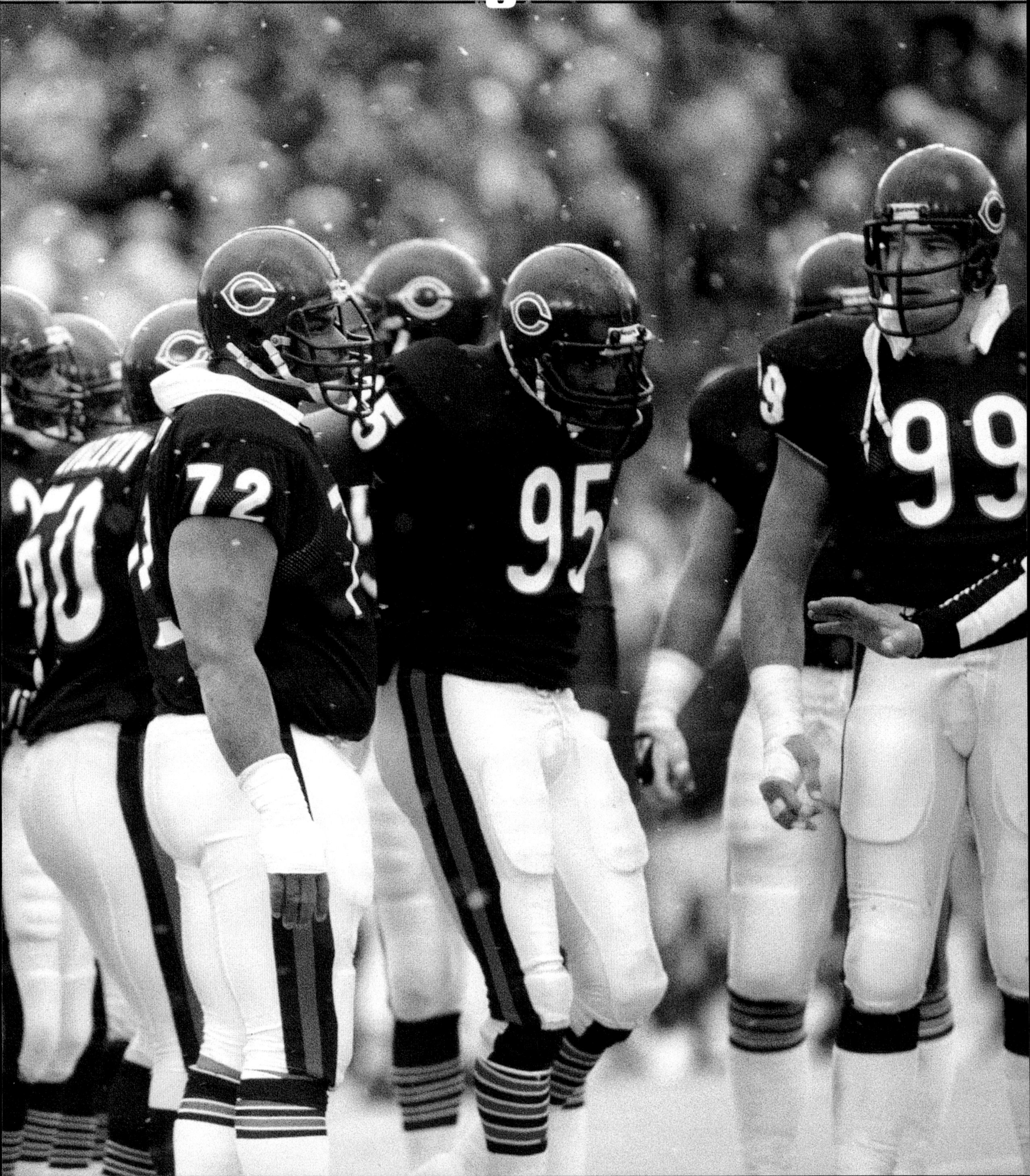

As good as the '85 Bears were, the team will be remembered most for its novel personalities. At quarterback, there was Jim McMahon (right), the punk-rock quarterback with the free spirit. On the defensive line, and sometimes in the offensive backfield, there was The Refrigerator, William Perry (below), a 350-pound package everyone could root for.

the New York Giants. The Bears were so cocksure about Super Bowl XX that more than a dozen players recorded and taped a rap song and video, "The Super Bowl Shuffle," with a month still to play in the regular season. They sold almost a million copies of the song and 200,000 copies of the videocassette, with the proceeds going to a charity to help feed the hungry.

And if there was a provocative headline to make, they made it. The usual suspect was Jim McMahon, the brash young quarterback with rolled-up uniform sleeves and a punk haircut. During one of

the Bears' practice sessions several days before the Super Bowl, McMahon mooned a helicopter hovering over the Bears' practice field. Headlines. Leading up to the big game, McMahon wanted the team to fly his personal acupuncturist to New Orleans to treat a bruise to his buttocks. When management refused, Hiroshi Shiriashi flew down compliments of the Illinois State Acupuncture Association. Headlines. McMahon allegedly referred to the women of New Orleans as "sluts" and the city's men as "idiots" on a radio show. He denied it. Didn't matter. Headlines.

Earlier in the season, McMahon and running back Walter Payton took on the NFL's button-down front office by flouting an order from commissioner Pete Rozelle to stop wearing headbands sporting their shoe company's name. When Rozelle fined the team $5,000 for that repeated transgression of the league's rules about uniforms, McMahon wrote the commissioner's name in big, bold letters on a couple of white headbands. In an act of civil disobedience that resonated across America, he and Payton wore them during the 24-0

NFC Championship Game victory over the L.A. Rams.

Among the other captivating Bears in 1985 was a 350-plus-pound rookie defensive tackle nicknamed "The Refrigerator." William Perry, whose gap-toothed smile and easy wit made him a darling of the media, added a dimension to the game rarely before seen in the NFL. In short-yardage situations, coach Mike Ditka occasionally sent the massive lineman into the offensive backfield to block, or even tote and catch the ball himself. "The Refrigerator" scored three touchdowns, two by run and one by pass, during the regular season.

But those shenanigans wouldn't have created the craze they did if the Bears hadn't been so dominating on the field. They cakewalked past their first 12 opponents and appeared to be on their way to duplicating the unbeaten (17-0) season put together 13 years earlier by the Miami Dolphins.

The domination came from that funny defense, which grew more and more imposing as the season unfolded. Ryan called it the "46" because one of his former players, Bears' safety Doug Plank, had worn that uniform number. The "46" defense featured eight players on the line of scrimmage, an unusual

Mike Singletary and Richard Dent were key figures in Buddy Ryan's famed "46" defense.

While the Bears had their share of personalities, they also had talent. None was better than Walter Payton, the player they called "Sweetness."

The Bears' offense was directed by McMahon, and linebacker Singletary (below) rekindled memories of Dick Butkus.

alignment that rendered many an offense's blocking schemes useless.

From that formation, Chicago could send any combination of linemen (ends Richard Dent and Dan Hampton, and tackles Steve McMichael and Perry), linebackers (Mike Singletary, Otis Wilson and Wilber Marshall), and defensive backs at a quarterback. The "46" ranked first in the league in points allowed, rushing yards allowed, total yards allowed, first downs allowed, pass-completion percentage, interceptions and turnovers.

The effectiveness of the novel defense may have been the cannon that shot Chicago to greatness, but the Bears had an above-average arsenal on the other side of the ball, too. They scored more points (456, an average of 28.5 per game) than any team in the league except the San Diego Chargers of Dan Fouts, Lionel James and Charlie Joiner.

Payton, one of the classiest running backs the NFL has known, gained 1,551 yards, third-best in the NFL in 1985. McMahon finished in the top 10 in the league in passing efficiency, and wide receiver Willie Gault had the best yardage-per-catch average

Safety Gary Fencik, like the entire Bears' defense, was ferocious against both the run and pass.

(21.3) in the NFC. Place-kicker Kevin Butler's 144 points led the league.

The Bears rolled through the first three-quarters of the season undefeated at 12-0, and then headed to Miami for a December 2 showdown on Monday night against the Dolphins. Miami's coach, Don Shula, had steered the Dolphins to their perfect 17-0 season in 1972, and he made an issue that night of protecting his favorite team's place in NFL history.

It worked. The Bears came into the game on the heels of consecutive shutouts of Dallas (44-0) and Atlanta (36-0), but Miami scored on every possession in the first half and led 31-10 at halftime. Meanwhile, the Dolphins' defense came up with three interceptions, a fumble recovery and six sacks. Despite Payton's eighth straight 100-plus-yard rushing game, Chicago suffered its first, and only, loss of the year, 38-24. The legacy of the '72 Dolphins was safe.

The Bears were too good, too strong and too fun-loving to need a wake-up call, but the loss to Miami strengthened their resolve to keep their magnificent season from slipping away. They dispatched their final three opponents, and then stormed through the postseason. Neither the Giants nor the Rams had a prayer in the NFC playoffs. Chicago outscored them by a total of 45-0.

In the Super Bowl, Chicago actually fell behind the Patriots, 3-0, less than a minute and a half into the game after McMahon and Payton fumbled a handoff on their own 19-yard line. But by halftime, the planets were back in alignment and Chicago led 23-3. A 21-point third quarter erased any lingering doubt, either about the game's outcome or the Bears' place as one of the great teams of all time.

Against the "46" defense, the Patriots managed a "grand" total of 7 rushing yards and 123 total yards.

And wouldn't you know it? The last touchdown of Chicago's most magnificent season was scored by "Refrigerator" Perry, the defensive tackle, on a 1-yard lumber over left guard.

Those were the Bears of 1985. Non-comformists until the end.

Coach Mike Ditka was on top of the world after the Bears earned their special niche in football history.

5

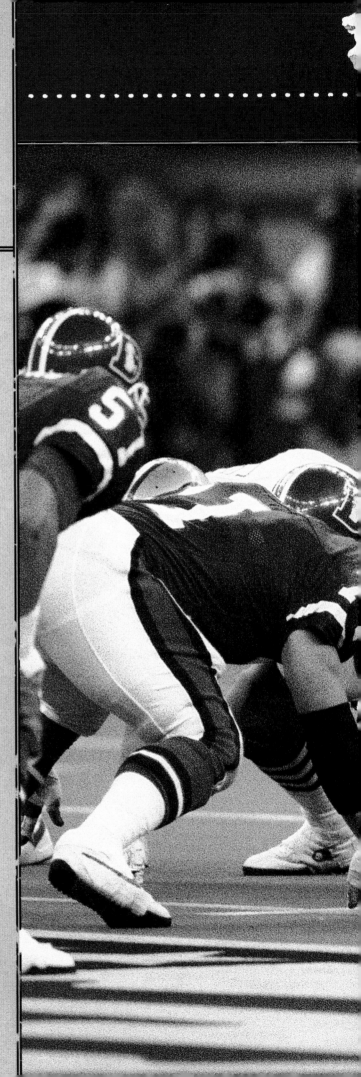

It was as if the National Football League let the other 27 teams play just for the sake of appearances. There was really only one team in 1989: San Francisco, playing in a league of its own. The rest of the NFL seemed to exist only because the 49ers had to play somebody.

Joe Montana had to throw touchdown passes against somebody.

Jerry Rice and John Taylor had to catch those passes against somebody.

Roger Craig and Tom Rathman had to run, block and catch Montana's swing passes against somebody.

So the NFL was kind enough to let those somebodies suit up every weekend. A couple of "other" teams actually managed to beat the 49ers, but the Rams' 13-12 victory in the fourth week of the season and Green Bay's 21-17 win seven weeks later did not fool anybody.

The Rams' win? They recovered a 49ers' fumble in the final few minutes, ran out the clock and kicked a game-winning field goal with two seconds left, denying Montana an opportunity to engineer one of his celebrated last-chance comebacks. Give "Joe Cool" last dibs on the ball, and the outcome likely is different. And the Packers? They needed 35 yards worth of San Francisco penalties, including an offsides call that nullified a 94-yard interception return for an apparent touchdown, to keep their winning drive going.

Joe Montana (16) dismantled the Broncos' defense in Super Bowl XXIV, completing 22-of-29 passes for 297 yards and five touchdowns.

It was not uncommon to see defenders tripping over themselves while trying to cover Jerry Rice.

San Francisco was clearly the class of the league, and everybody knew it.

The 49ers had been running Bill Walsh's version of the West Coast offense since 1979. It had already helped San Francisco to Super Bowl victories after the 1981, 1984 and 1988 seasons. In '89, now under first-year head coach George Seifert and quarterbacks coach Mike Holmgren, the offense reached a new level of production and efficiency.

It was close to unstoppable. Montana, who had been with the 49ers from the beginning of Walsh's tenure, had a decade of experience with the lightning-quick timing of the West Coast attack. Backward, forward, upside and down, he knew every intricacy of the offense's underneath crossing routes, its swing passes and its ability to force slow-footed linebackers into mismatched coverage on fleet backs and wide receivers.

Montana had been marvelous with the offense throughout the '80s. In 1989, "marvelous" didn't begin to describe his flair for making it work. The season played out like a hit television series. The Joe Montana Show kept topping itself.

He passed for 428 yards and five touchdowns against the Eagles.

For 302 yards and three touchdowns against New Orleans.

For 292 yards and three touchdowns against the Giants on 27 completions in 33 attempts, an incredible completion percentage of .818.

For 270 yards and three more TDs with an even better completion percentage (.842, on a 16-for-19 performance) against Atlanta.

For 325 yards and a pair of scores in the loss to Green Bay.

For 458 yards and three touchdowns in the second game against the Rams, avenging the early-season loss to L.A. in which he'd "only" passed for 227 yards on 25 completions in 35 attempts with no interceptions.

At the end of the regular season, Montana had thrown for 3,521 yards and 26 touchdowns, with only eight interceptions. His most impressive statistic, though, was his completion percentage. He put the ball in the air 386 times; one of

his teammates came down with it 271 times. That's a 70.2-percent success rate.

The NFL began tracking quarterback passing efficiency with a complicated rating system in 1973, factoring together completion percentage, yards gained, touchdown passes and interception percentage. Before 1989, the highest-rated quarterback in any single season had been Dan Marino in 1984. His 5,084 yards and 48 touchdown passes gave him a rating of 108.9.

Montana bettered it in '89, with a quarterback rating of 112.4. Only once since then has anybody surpassed that number. Steve Young, Montana's backup with the 49ers in 1989, steered San Francisco's West Coast offense to even greater heights in 1994 with a rating of 112.8.

The '89 version of the West Coast offense consisted of parts that seemed born to play it. Rice and Taylor gave Montana and Young a pair of big, fast wide receivers who could stretch a defense and leave the

> The season played out like a hit television series. The Joe Montana Show kept topping itself.

Roger Craig (left) and Tom Rathman were the ideal backs for the West Coast offense—they could catch the ball as well as run with it.

short zones unprotected. Rice caught 17 touchdown passes on 82 receptions for 1,483 yards; Taylor had 10 TD catches among his 60 receptions for 1,077 yards. Brent Jones, the tight end, caught another 40 passes for 500 yards.

For much of its success, the offense depends on backs who can catch the ball as well as carry it.

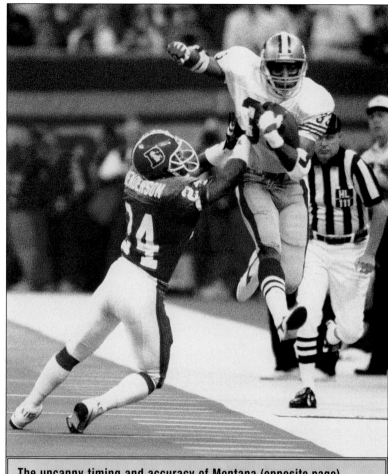

The uncanny timing and accuracy of Montana (opposite page) complemented such ever-reliable receivers as Craig (above).

Rathman and Craig combined for 122 catches and 1,089 yards in receptions out of the backfield. As potent as the passing game was, the 49ers balanced it with 1,054 rushing yards from Craig and the short-yardage certainty of Rathman, the fullback.

And, of course, Montana made it all happen with his mastery of the quick reads the offense requires and his unparalleled touch on the timing passes it employs.

Put all that together, and the 49ers' offense could move the ball in more ways than defenses could prepare to stop.

Conversely, San Francisco's own defense, which was good at the beginning of the season, became great by the end. Two significant personnel changes made the 1989 defense more physical than the group that had given up an average of just 18.4 points per game in San Francisco's Super Bowl season of '88. First, Seifert signed inside linebacker Matt Millen, who had been released by the Raiders near the end of training camp. Then, when strong safety Jeff Fuller suffered a spinal injury against New England in the seventh game of '89, Chet Brooks moved into the starting spot.

Millen and Brooks added muscle and a presence to an already-solid group. In 1989, San Francisco knocked more than two points a game off the average it had allowed a year earlier. Only the Broncos and the Giants gave up fewer points.

By the end of the year, the 49ers had a head of steam that flat vaporized the other aspirants to the Super Bowl title. Starting with a 26-0 thumping of Chicago in the last game of the regular season, San Francisco outscored its final four opponents by a combined 152-26.

The 49ers humbled Minnesota in the first round of the playoffs, 41-13, as Montana completed 17 of his 24 passes for 241 yards and four touchdowns.

In the NFC Championship Game against the Rams, he was 26-of-30—an astonishing

Charles Haley (94 above) and Ronnie Lott (below) led a defensive unit that allowed 15.8 points per game.

86.7-percent completion rate—for 262 yards and two touchdowns.

His best came last. In Super Bowl XXIV, the Broncos opened with their safeties in a two-deep zone, which left the middle of the field wide open for Rice and Taylor. Of course, Denver's other option was to try to cover Rice and Taylor man-to-man, which would have been asking for miracles from journeyman cornerbacks Tyrone Braxton and Wymon Henderson.

By the end of the third quarter, Montana had thrown five touchdown passes. Rice caught three of them, and Taylor and Jones one apiece. Two of Rice's TD catches, as well as Taylor's 35-yard scoring reception, came straight down the middle of Denver's secondary.

Montana finished with 297 yards, the five touchdowns and his third Super Bowl MVP

trophy. Only seven of his 29 passes were incomplete; none of them was intercepted. San Francisco totally overmatched the Broncos, 55-10.

Even at the Super Bowl, it was as if the 49ers were the only team playing.

John Taylor (82) was a frequent recipient of Montana touchdown passes—as he was in the Super Bowl.

6

The mighty National Football League asked for it, over and over again, with braggadocio like this: "Come back when you get a football," NFL commissioner Bert Bell told the owners of the All-America Football Conference (AAFC) in 1946.

"The worst team in our league could beat the best team in theirs," Washington Redskins owner George Preston Marshall said about the AAFC in 1949.

"The high school kids are coming to play the pros," Philadelphia Eagles coach Greasy Neale said about the merger with the AAFC heading into the 1950 season.

You shouldn't mess with Paul Brown like that. You shouldn't mess with the Cleveland Browns like that.

So when the NFL finally admitted three of the AAFC franchises (Cleveland, Baltimore and San Francisco) into the fold in 1950, Brown and the team named after him already had the Establishment square in their sights.

The Browns had dominated the AAFC during all four of its seasons, winning the title each year. In their last 38 AAFC games, they had gone 35-1-2. So they were good. Very good.

But few NFL officials, coaches or players wanted to believe it.

So they kept asking for it. And Cleveland kept giving it to them. In the process, the Browns humbled an entire league.

They started with a special Saturday night opener against Neale's defending NFL champion Eagles, a game scheduled before the rest of the league kicked off so a

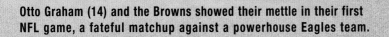

Otto Graham (14) and the Browns showed their mettle in their first NFL game, a fateful matchup against a powerhouse Eagles team.

1950 Cleveland Browns

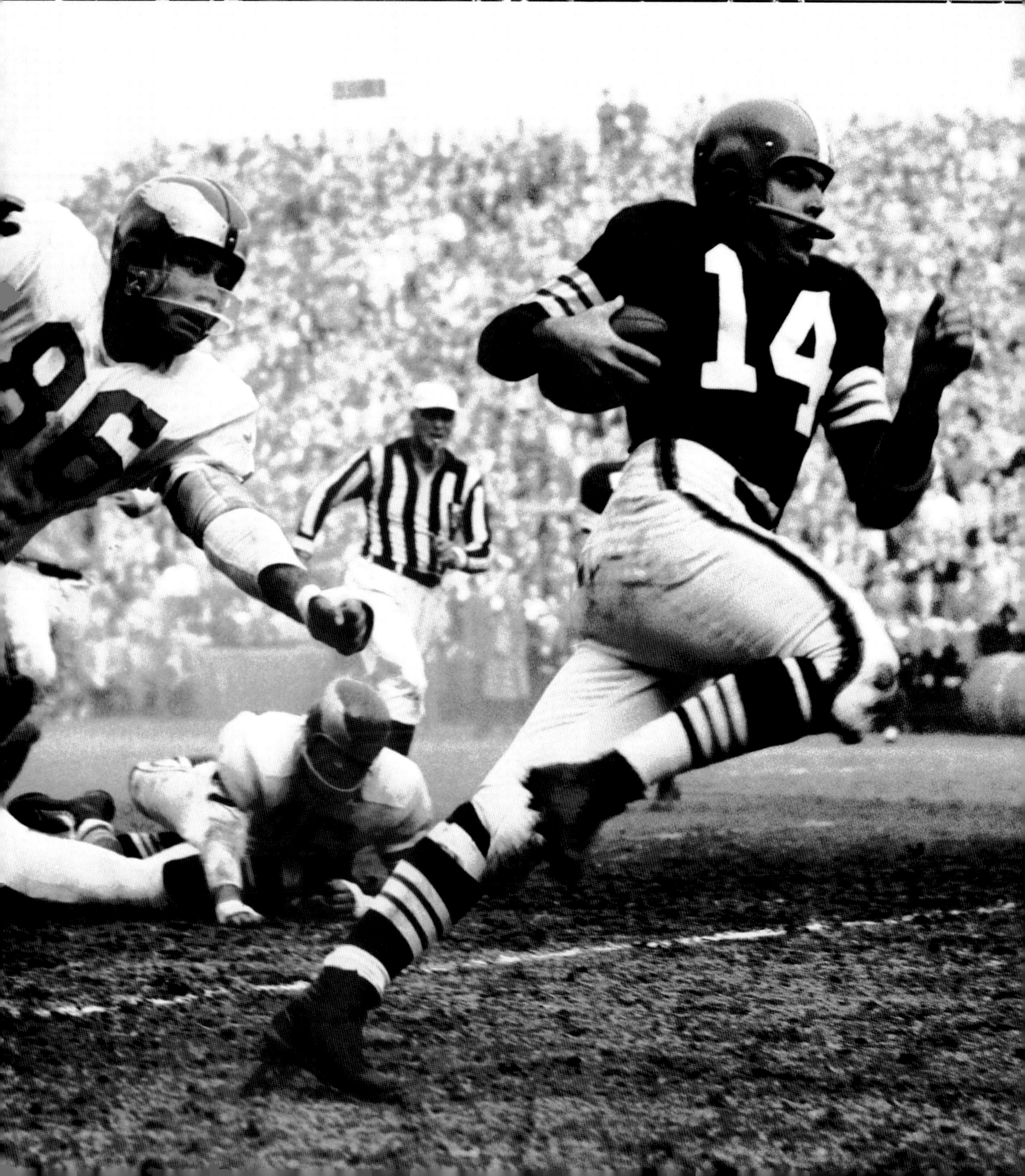

greater number of fans could be made aware of the comeuppance the established league would give to the upstarts from Cleveland.

In most cases, the last game of the season, the championship game, is what cements a team's claim to its place among the best of all time. But for the Browns of 1950, that first game, the one in Philadelphia's Municipal Stadium in front of 71,237 Eagles partisans, did more to immortalize the team than anything else during its 12-2 wild ride of a season.

They utterly whipped the defending-champ Eagles, 35-10, that night.

Philadelphia came into the 1950 season featuring Neale's famous and physical "Eagle" defense, a 5-2-4 alignment that put four defensive backs up close to the line of scrimmage and had linebackers playing outside to rough up the offensive ends. That defense, along with a powerful running game featuring halfback Steve Van Buren out of the "wing T" formation, had helped fashion an 11-1 record for Philadelphia in 1949 and a 14-0 shutout of the Rams in the championship game.

Brown wasn't fazed. Knowing an AAFC merger with the NFL was inevitable, he'd been scouting the Eagles for the two years prior to 1950. He had his quarterback, Otto Graham, throw a series of passes on flare and sideline routes to capitalize on mismatches in speed on the outside. The Eagles' outside linebackers, forced to play man-to-man coverage, couldn't keep up with the fleet feet of Mac Speedie, Dub Jones and Dante Lavelli. Graham threw for 346 yards and two touchdowns on 21 completions in 38 attempts.

As soon as Philadelphia began to show signs that it was adjusting to Cleveland's passing game, Brown spread the Eagles' defense by extending the gaps between his offensive linemen, and turned the game over to his 238-pound fullback, Marion Motley.

It was a brilliant game plan, and it stuck in Neale's craw. Afterward, the Eagles' coach groused long and loud about Graham's 38 passes, intimating that the Browns had played something less than a physical game.

In other words, the NFL, in the form of Neale, asked for it again. When Cleveland played the Eagles in a rematch later that season, Graham only threw one pass, a completion that

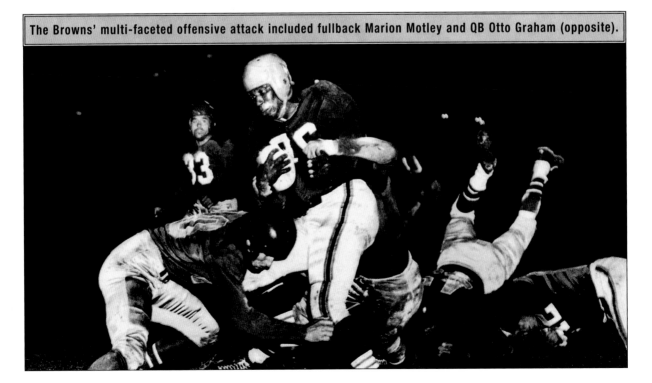

The Browns' multi-faceted offensive attack included fullback Marion Motley and QB Otto Graham (opposite).

Coach Paul Brown (center) and the team named in his honor celebrate their championship win over the Rams.

was nullified by a penalty. Every other play was a run. The wet, muddy field on a cold early-December day in Cleveland had as much to do with that game plan as Neale's "fightin' words"; but, nonetheless, the Browns couldn't have been more physical. And they won again, 13-7.

If anything, the Browns' season-opening rout of the defending NFL champs made them even more of a target. Now the rest of the league was determined to teach the newcomers what Philadelphia couldn't.

But only one team had the right stuff to beat the Browns. The New York Giants and their coach, Steve Owen, dreamed up a defensive wrinkle two weeks after the first Eagles' game and shut Cleveland out, 6-0. Until then, no Paul Brown-coached team had ever been held scoreless. The Giants used a 6-1-4 alignment that day, an innovative "Umbrella Defense" that was the precursor of the 4-3 defense. By dropping two ends into pass coverage along with the four defensive backs, New York held Graham without a completion in the first half.

When the Giants and the Browns played again several weeks later, Owen used an extra man in the secondary (a "nickel" back, in today's terminology) and beat Cleveland again, this time by a 17-13 score.

Those were the Browns' only two losses. And as it happened, they finished the regular season in a deadlock with the Giants at 10-2, necessitating a third game against New York for the right to play for the NFL championship.

This time, on a slick, frozen field in 10-degree temperature in Cleveland, the Browns' defense excelled. In that weather, Giants quarterback Charlie Conerly completed only three passes (Graham was just as ineffective) and the two teams entered the final minute tied, 3-3. With 58 seconds left, Lou Groza kicked a 28-yard field goal to put

Cleveland up, 6-3.

Linebacker Bill Willis, who saved a touchdown earlier in the fourth quarter when he caught the Giants' Eugene "Choo Choo" Roberts at the 4-yard line, tackled Conerly in the end zone for a safety in the closing seconds, and the Browns were on their way to the title game with an 8-3 victory.

The Browns had arrived. About that, there could be no doubt. Motley led the league in rushing with 810 yards. Groza kicked a league-record 13 field goals. And Paul Brown's innovative sideline and screen passes, thrown by Graham and featuring elements of today's "West Coast" offense, revolutionized football's passing attacks.

But there was still one more hurdle: Los Angeles, for the championship. In a way, the Rams were the perfect team for Cleveland's final in-your-face answer to all of the NFL's belittlement of its AAFC heritage. Until 1946, the Rams had called Cleveland home; but despite winning the league title in 1945, owner Dan Reeves pulled out of the city and moved his franchise to California.

The 1950 championship game was the first time the Rams had played in Cleveland's Municipal Stadium since that abrupt departure. Again, the weather was abysmal, bitterly cold and windy. The Rams came out in traditional football cleats. The Browns wore high-topped sneakers for better traction.

Los Angeles led 28-20 after three quarters, but Graham moved the Browns 65 yards with nine completions, capping the drive with a touchdown pass to Rex Bumgardner to make the score 28-27 late in the fourth period. Cleveland took possession for the final time with 1:48 to play, 68 yards from the end zone.

Eighty seconds later, Graham had his team on the Rams' 11-yard line. Another Groza field goal gave the Browns the game and the NFL championship, 30-28.

The NFL had asked for it. The Browns gave it in spades.

As Dante Lavelli delivers an in-your-face block, Otto Graham cuts through

T wo stories from Super Bowl I illuminate the success of the 1966 champion Green Bay Packers.

The first story is a song, a tune hummed by guard Fred "Fuzzy" Thurston in the fourth quarter of the Packers' 35-10 victory over the Chiefs. There was a break in the action on the field, a hiatus caused by the impact of Green Bay running back Donny Anderson's knee on Kansas City cornerback Fred Williamson's helmet. Williamson was knocked out cold in the collision. The kayo wasn't the only problem for the man known as "The Hammer." Kansas City linebacker Sherrill Headrick, speeding in to help on the tackle, dived into the heap of players and broke Williamson's arm.

Leading up to the game, "The Hammer" had yakked long and loud about how he planned to aim his trademark forearm whacks at the heads of Green Bay's backs and receivers. It was trash talk, ahead of its heyday. The Packers hadn't responded. But as Williamson was carried off the field on a stretcher with his team behind by three touchdowns and a field goal, Thurston was heard warbling the Peter, Paul and Mary hit, "If I Had a Hammer."

The '66 Packers played even the biggest of games with that kind of quiet smugness.

And why not? Going into the Super Bowl, Green Bay had already won four of the seven NFL championships decided in the '60s to that point. In 1966, the Packers coasted to a 12-2 regular-season record. With another field goal here and an extra point there, they might have been a perfect 14-0. Their two losses were by one point (21-20) to San Francisco and three points (20-17) to Minnesota.

Against the upstart Chiefs from the American Football

Bart Starr grabbed MVP honors while leading the Packers to victory in Super Bowl I with 250 yards passing and two touchdowns.

Starr finished the regular season with 14 TD passes and only three interceptions.

touring Hollywood's hotspots. How he had stumbled into the hotel lobby at 7:30 in the morning and bumped into Bart Starr as Starr came down for breakfast. How just before the 1 p.m. kickoff, Paul Hornung had joked with him on the sidelines about playing with a hangover. How Dowler had separated his shoulder on the second play of the game. How McGee had been forced into action.

And how he had caught seven passes for 138 yards and two touchdowns, including the first score in Super Bowl history.

But you may not remember McGee's contribution to the 1966 Green Bay Packers two weeks before the Super Bowl. You may not remember how with 5:20 to play in the NFL Championship Game against Dallas—the game the Packers had to win to advance to the Super Bowl—McGee caught the winning touchdown pass.

That's the pass that put Green Bay ahead of the Cowboys 34-20, a lead the Packers barely salvaged with an end-zone interception by strong safety Tom Brown of a Don Meredith pass from the 2-yard line with 28 seconds left and the score 34-27.

McGee may not have been a model citizen cut from the cloth of Vince Lombardi's ideal, but he was always ready to play. Even when he least expected to.

So were the rest of the Packers, which is one of the reasons their stay at the top of pro football lasted as long as it did. In 1966, the sailing was anything but smooth in Green Bay, but Lombardi's famous preparation and preachy precepts always seemed to steer the team through the storms.

Before the season had begun, star fullback Jim Taylor told the team that he intended to play out the last year of his contract and sign with the expansion New Orleans Saints, who were to debut in 1967. Taylor was born in Louisiana. He went to high school in Louisiana. He went to college at Louisiana State. His desire to finish his career in New

League, Green Bay played with the maturity and composure fostered by the franchise's proud tradition. It didn't hurt, of course, that the '66 Packers had the best defense in the NFL. The '66 Packers may have been slower of foot and longer of tooth than the Green Bay team that won the NFL championship in 1962, but they were still better than the rest and they knew it.

So Thurston hummed away.

The second story is the celebrated saga of Max McGee. You've probably heard this one. How McGee had only caught four passes during the regular season as a backup to Boyd Dowler. How he didn't expect to play against the Chiefs. How he had decided to retire as soon as the season ended. How he had stayed out all night the night before the Super Bowl

Despite a dispute with coach Vince Lombardi, Jim Taylor still carried the Packers' running load.

Orleans made perfect sense.

Didn't matter. Lombardi was furious. Taylor and his coach didn't speak all season. But that didn't stop Lombardi from getting the most out of one of the best all-around offensive players in football. Taylor led the Packers in both rushing (705 yards) and receiving (41 catches).

Then there was Hornung, who was at the end of his career but still an integral part of the Packers. Hornung was the halfback, still a force on the famed Packer sweep and still a threat to throw an option pass . . . when he was healthy. Hornung, though, wasn't healthy down the stretch. He didn't play in the Super Bowl because of a pinched nerve in his neck.

But Lombardi had the backfield ready with Elijah Pitts and his two high-priced rookies,

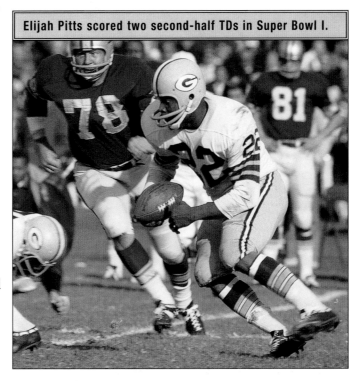

Elijah Pitts scored two second-half TDs in Super Bowl I.

Anderson and Jim Grabowski (known as the Gold Dust Twins for their big contracts). Pitts scored two of Green Bay's three touchdowns in the second half of the Super Bowl as the Packers pulled away from a 14-10 halftime lead to win easily.

The year was busy with adjustments. Perhaps the most significant was the offensive adjustment the Packers made to play the Cowboys in the postseason. Lombardi had always been a run-first-and-pass-later coach, and that hadn't changed during the regular season. But as he prepared to face Dallas, the best passing team in the NFL, Lombardi realized he could win a shootout.

He had the most efficient quarterback in the league in Starr, who threw 14 touchdown passes against only three interceptions that season. Meredith,

the Redskins' Sonny Jurgensen and several others had amassed better yardage and more TDs, but Starr didn't make mistakes. And Lombardi knew the Cowboys' defense had focused its preparation on stopping the run.

So suddenly, Green Bay became a passing team. Starr threw four touchdown passes against Dallas, including a 51-yard bomb to Carroll Dale and the 28-yard game-winner to McGee. It was a masterstroke of coaching.

As the Chiefs prepared for the Super Bowl, they also concentrated on stopping the Packers' running game. Lombardi's track record with it was impossible to ignore. As

> **The quarterback was named the game's most valuable player, but the award might easily have gone to McGee.**

the game unfolded, Kansas City appeared to have made the right guess. Green Bay ran the ball 33 times, right on their average during the regular season. Starr threw 23 passes, which also was close to his standard number that year.

The difference? Maybe it was that the Chiefs didn't prepare to cover McGee. Starr completed 16 of his 23 passes, including the seven to McGee, for 250 yards and the two touchdowns. The quarterback was named the game's most valuable player, but the award might easily have gone to McGee.

What a story, and what a party, that would have made.

The Packers' defense, which featured linebackers Nitschke and Dave Robinson (89), was the best in the NFL.

The National Football League had never experienced a more exceptional season for offense. If there was a scoring, passing, rushing or receiving record to be broken, it seemed as if somebody took center stage in 1984.

Defense? In 1984, the league played defense as if it were an afterthought.

Except in San Francisco. When they played against San Francisco, most of the league's offensive stars took giant steps backward on their way to record heights. The 49ers faced, and stopped, a remarkable number of the best and the brightest quarterbacks, running backs and receivers the NFL has ever seen.

Of course, San Francisco featured its own remarkable offense, too. The 49ers scored more points (475) in 1984 than any team except the high-flying passing machine led by Dan Marino in Miami. When they beat the Dolphins, 38-16, for the league championship, the 49ers set a team Super Bowl record with 537 net yards, and quarterback Joe Montana set an individual Super Bowl mark with 331 passing yards.

But the better part of the credit for San Francisco's 15-1 regular-season record and Super Bowl XIX title goes to a defense that met and passed challenge after imposing challenge.

Some of the league's 1984 stars and record-breakers, and how they fared against the 49ers:

• The Rams' Eric Dickerson shattered O.J. Simpson's single-season rushing record by gaining

Joe Montana (16) was masterful in 1984, whether tossing quick passes or handing off to Roger Craig (33).

2,105 yards, an average of 131.5 per game. He played against San Francisco twice in NFC Western Division games. In the first meeting, he gained 38 yards on 13 carries, a per-carry average of 2.9 yards. Not surprisingly, the 49ers shut L.A. out, 33-0. Dickerson played a little better in the second game, a 19-16 San Francisco victory in the regular-season finale. But with 98 yards on 26 carries (3.8 yards per carry), he was still far below his average. He scored a league-high 14 rushing touchdowns that year, but only one of them came in the two 49er games.

• In October of '84, the Bears' Walter Payton broke Jim Brown's career rushing record of 12,312 yards. Payton had one of his best seasons with 1,684 yards and 11 touchdowns. But when he ran into San Francisco's defense in the NFC title game, his numbers were ordinary. He carried 22 times for 92 yards and didn't score. Neither did any of the other Bears. The 49ers won, 23-0.

• Tampa Bay running back James Wilder rushed for 1,544 yards and set a league record

Ronnie Lott was one of the hardest hitters in the game.

for carries with 407, an average of 25.4 per game. On November 18, San Francisco forced the Buccaneers into a come-from-behind passing game that limited Wilder to 18 rushes for 89 yards and no touchdowns. The 49ers won, 24-17.

• In the eight games Detroit's Billy Sims played in '84 before he tore up a knee, he went over 100 yards rushing four times and averaged 5.3 yards per carry. The Lions opened their season at home against San Francisco. Sims carried 17 times for a ho-hum 69 yards. The 49ers won, 30-27.

• John Riggins gained 1,239 yards and scored 14 touchdowns for the Redskins in '84. It was his second-best season, coming on the heels of a 1983 performance in which he gained 1,347 yards and scored 24 times. Washington played at San Francisco in the second game of the year. In a wild one, the 49ers won 37-31. Riggins? He carried 10 times and gained 12 yards, although he scored twice from short yardage.

• Riggins didn't set any records in 1984, but another Redskin did. Wide receiver Art

Monk broke a 20-year-old single-season mark by catching 106 passes. Monk is the one record-breaker the 49ers didn't contain that year. Against San Francisco, he had 10 receptions for 200 yards. None of those receptions, though, was for a touchdown.

All of the 49ers' defensive success during the regular season and into the playoffs was merely a prologue for the predicament San Francisco faced in Super Bowl XIX. Miami brought Marino and one of the most prolific offenses in NFL history to Stanford Stadium for the Super Bowl. Before 1984, the league had never experienced the kind of passing onslaught the Dolphins inflicted on opponents. Nobody had ever thrown for more yardage (5,084), more completions (362) or more touchdowns (48) in a single season than Marino did in '84. Nor had anyone ever caught more touchdown passes than Mark Clayton did with 18.

The 49ers didn't stop Marino & Co. cold, but San Francisco certainly controlled them. Defensive coordinator George Seifert dreamed up two wrinkles specifically for the occasion. Both of them worked well enough to keep Marino from establishing the consis-

Bill Walsh was the brainchild of an offense that used the skills of Montana and Craig (below).

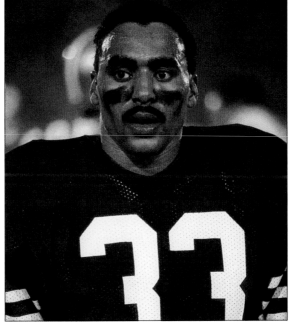

tent rhythm that had led Miami to an NFL-high average of 32.1 points per game.

Seifert's first adjustment involved his defensive front. He installed a new set of linemen-and-linebacker stunts to pressure and confuse Dolphins' center Dwight Stephenson. Miami's offensive line had been nearly impeccable at pass protection throughout the season. Marino had been sacked only 13 times, an extraordinarily low number for a quarterback who threw 564 passes. But with Stephenson and guards Roy Foster and Ed Newman occupied by the new-look pass rush, the 49ers found lanes leading to Miami's backfield. They sacked Marino four times.

Still, the Dolphins' passing game clicked early. Marino completed nine of his first 10 passes and Miami led 10-7 in the first quarter. So in the second quarter, Seifert went to a fifth, and then a sixth man in the secondary. Four of his defensive backs played man-to-man coverage, with two more safeties staying deep in a zone. The nickel-and-dime defenses kept the Dolphins scoreless in the second half.

Marino threw 50 passes and completed 29 for 318 yards, which was exactly his per-game

The combination of Wendell Tyler (above) and Montana (opposite page) made the 49ers virtually unstoppable.

average during the regular season. But he'd been on such a roll coming into the Super Bowl that those 318 yards were his second-lowest total in Miami's last six games. And his only touchdown pass was to tight end Dan Johnson.

Forced to play from behind after San Francisco's 21-point second quarter, the Dolphins totally abandoned their already-mediocre running game. They finished with 25 net yards on the ground.

The 49ers' strong defensive performance meant Montana & Co. didn't need to be spectacular to win. But they were. The Dolphins set their defense to take away San Francisco's deep routes, which played perfectly into the short passing game that was the strength of Bill Walsh's West Coast offense. Montana completed 24 of his 35 passes for three touchdowns and 331 yards, and scrambled five times for another 59 yards and a fourth TD.

The 49ers and Montana had won Super Bowl XVI over Cincinnati three years

earlier with an offense that was just learning how potent it could be. By 1984, the West Coast offense had added a pair of big, versatile and sure-handed running backs in Wendell Tyler (1,262 rushing yards and 28 receptions) and Roger Craig (649 yards on the ground and 71 catches). It had matured into a dominating force that came up four points and a few minutes short of a perfect season. San Francisco's only loss came to Pittsburgh in the seventh week, when Gary Anderson's field goal in the closing moments gave the Steelers a 20-17 win.

They were, indeed, a star-studded offense, those 49ers, in a season chock-full of stars throughout the league. But Montana, Tyler, Craig, Dwight Clark, Freddie Solomon, Russ Francis and San Francisco's other offensive playmakers had one very big advantage over the rest of the NFL in 1984.

They didn't have to play against the 49ers' defense.

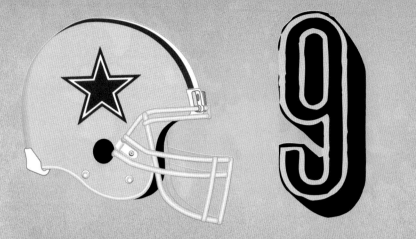

T he Cowboys were one game better during the 1977 regular season— one game better than their 11-3 record of a year earlier. But that one-game difference in the standings does not begin to tell the story of the leaps and bounds by which Dallas improved on both sides of the line of scrimmage on its way to a Super Bowl XII victory over Denver.

A little game of NFL trivia will help track those leaps. The answers to two esoteric questions provide some clues to the bounds.

Question No. 1: What do Walter Payton, Chuck Foreman and Otis Armstrong have in common?

Yes, they were all great NFL running backs. And yes, they were all 1,000-yard rushers during the decade of the '70s. But the correct answer, for these purposes, is that all three of them were stopped stone-cold in successive postseason games by the 1977 Cowboys' Doomsday II Defense.

Dallas started the playoffs against Payton's Bears. Chicago was 9-5 and the NFC's wild-card team in '77. Not a powerhouse. Still, Payton was the NFL's leading rusher with 1,852 yards, the third-highest total in NFL history, and Chicago had the league's best overall ground game. Against the Cowboys, though, Payton ran nowhere fast. He managed only 60 yards and Dallas won, 37-7.

The next week, in the NFC Championship Game,

The Dallas defense featured Randy White (54) and Harvey Martin (79), who created a Doomsday atmosphere for opponents.

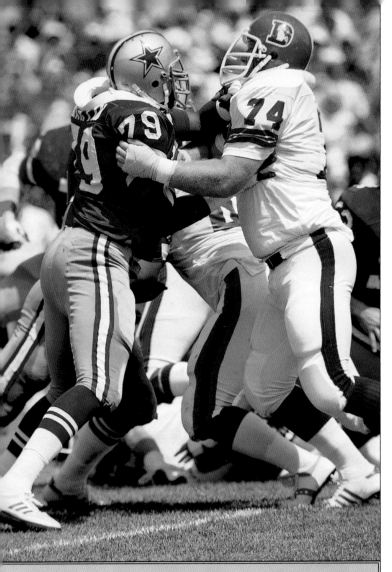

White (54 below) plugged the middle and Martin (79) anchored one end of an impenetrable defensive front wall.

the Cowboys played Foreman's Vikings. Minnesota, also 9-5, beat the Rams in its first-round playoff game behind 101 rushing yards from Foreman, who gained 1,112 during the regular season. But against Dallas, his 21 carries netted only 59 yards; and the Vikings as a team had just 66 yards on the ground as the Cowboys won, 23-6.

In the Super Bowl, Armstrong fared even more miserably. He had struggled through an injury-plagued 1977 season, gaining only 489 yards. But he'd rushed for 1,008 yards in 1976; and going into the Super Bowl, he was still the Broncos' best breakaway threat. The Cowboys held him to 27 yards on seven carries. Dallas danced, 27-10.

Neither Payton, Foreman nor Armstrong scored in those games. In fact, until Rob Lytle's meaningless second-half, 1-yard touchdown run in the Super Bowl after Dallas had a 20-3 lead, the Cowboys didn't give up a post-season rushing TD.

A year earlier, their run defense was good. But not that good. One of the reasons it improved was a training-camp decision to move Randy White from linebacker to defensive tackle. White immediately settled into the starting role and teamed with Harvey Martin, Jethro Pugh and Ed "Too Tall" Jones to make up one of the game's most impenetrable lines. White and middle linebacker Bob Breunig helped bring Tom Landry's Flex defense back to the standard the first Doomsday Defense had set during the Cowboys' Super Bowl season of 1971.

Landry pioneered the Flex in the '60s to stop the run, so it was a good match for the NFL's rush-happy offenses of the '70s. Two linemen took stances several yards off the line of scrimmage, which allowed them to react and flow to the direction of the play, while the other linemen held their positions at the point of attack to occupy blockers.

Because Landry was the only coach who used the Flex extensively, the Cowboys posed a singular problem as teams prepared to play them. The Bears, the Vikings and the Broncos found that out the hard way in the postseason.

In '77, Dallas led the NFC in fewest rushing yards allowed (117.9 per game) and the league in fewest total yards allowed (229.5 per game). Against that defense, the poor Broncos, who made it into their first Super Bowl on the strength of their "Orange Crush" defense rather than their offense, gained a grand total of 156 yards.

On to Question No. 2: What do Steve August, Tom Lynch, Terry Beeson and Pete Cronan have in common?

Answer: They were the players taken by Seattle in the 1977 draft with the four picks the Seahawks received from Dallas in exchange for the second overall choice.

With the pick Seattle traded away, the Cowboys drafted Tony Dorsett and immediately became one of the most potent offenses in the NFL. In his rookie season, Dorsett gained 1,007 yards and gave Dallas breakaway speed in the backfield, the one piece of the puzzle the offense was missing in 1976. That year, the Cowboys' leading rusher was Doug

Dennison, a plodder by comparison, who gained 542 yards.

Dorsett didn't get his first start until November 20 in the season's 10th game, which makes his 1,000-yard year and 13 touchdowns all the more remarkable.

In '77, Dallas finally had all the offensive ingredients—Roger Staubach, a seasoned, cagey quarterback who rarely made mistakes and mastered Landry's innovative shotgun formation; Drew Pearson and Golden Richards, speedsters at wide receiver; Billy Joe DuPree, a tight end with good hands and wheels; Preston Pearson, a back whose forté was the third-down reception; Robert Newhouse, the round little runner who paired with Dorsett; and, of course, "T.D." himself.

Defenses were still dominating throughout the NFL in the mid-'70s, even as league officials kept tinkering with the rules in attempts to open up the passing game. In 1977, defenders were allowed to make contact with receivers only once, and defensive linemen were no longer permitted to head-slap the men trying to block them. Those changes didn't help. There were fewer points scored across the league than in any

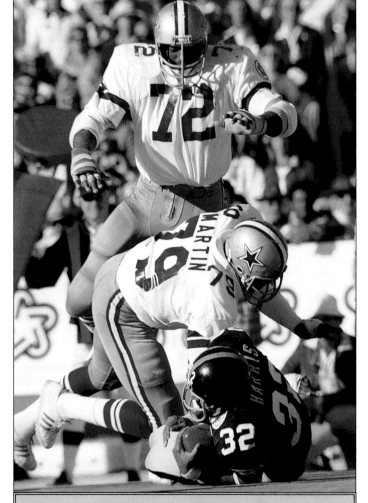

Not lost in the Doomsday defensive shuffle was Too Tall Jones (72), who towered over opponents.

season since 1942.

The Cowboys' offense, though, adapted to the new rules better than most teams. Only Oakland scored more than Dallas' 24.6 points-per-game average. That offense along with the rejuvenated Flex defense made the Cowboys the class of the league. They won their first eight games, even as Landry held Dorsett back until the rookie became comfortable with the intricate Dallas playbook.

The most impressive of those early wins came on October 16 at home against the Redskins. In that game, Dallas' balance was never better. The Cowboys gained 433 yards while they thoroughly throttled Billy Kilmer's offense. Washington netted 1 yard passing and gained an average of 1.7 yards per play.

After the 8-0 start, the Cowboys dropped their next two—a 24-17 loss to St. Louis and a 28-13 loss to Pittsburgh. But they finished the regular season with four consecutive victories, including a 14-6 win over Denver in the finale.

The Super Bowl rematch turned into a mismatch. Dorsett scored early on a 3-yard run and Efren Herrera kicked a pair of field goals to put Dallas up 13-0 at halftime. In the second half, reserve wide receiver Butch Johnson made a diving, finger-tip catch in the end zone of a 45-yard

Staubach bomb, and Newhouse threw his first pass of the season on a halfback option that went 29 yards to Richards for another

Quarterback Roger Staubach beat opponents with both his arm and legs.

touchdown.

The Broncos were so bamboozled by the Flex and by their first experience with the big-game atmosphere that they never came close to making a contest of it. White was too quick for Denver guard Tom Glassic, and Martin manhandled left tackle Andy Maurer. By halftime, Dallas had intercepted quarterback Craig Morton, an ex-Cowboy, four times.

Morton and backup quarterback Norris Weese, who played much of the second half, combined to complete only eight passes in 25 attempts for an unbelievably-low 35 net passing yards. Lytle was Denver's leading rusher in the game with a mere 35 yards on 10 carries; neither he nor Armstrong found any room to run.

In addition to the four early interceptions, the Cowboys also recovered four Denver fumbles and sacked Morton and Weese four times. Defensive back Randy Hughes accounted for three of the turnovers with two fumble recoveries and one of the interceptions. But White and Martin, the point men in Dallas' defensive attack, were named the game's co-MVPs.

The 'Boys were back. And better than ever.

Rookie Tony Dorsett gained 1,007 yards and gave the Dallas offense the one thing it lacked—speed.

Among the offensive weapons at coach Tom Landry's disposal were Golden Richards and Robert Newhouse.

10

T he Oakland Raiders waited until they were, oh, maybe 25 minutes into the 1976 season before they established themselves as intimidators. All it took was one George Atkinson forearm to the back of Lynn Swann's head during the September 12 season opener to set the tone.

Swann, Pittsburgh's third-year wide receiver, was playing his first game since being named the most valuable player of Super Bowl X. After the blow from Atkinson, he left the field with a concussion.

Atkinson, the strong safety, kept playing.

Eventually, Atkinson's wallet was $1,500 lighter, the size of his fine for the hit. He was forced to endure the pain and suffering of an official letter of reprimand from NFL commissioner Pete Rozelle, too. But he kept playing.

So the season had barely started and the Raiders were already on their way, not only to building on their reputation as some of the most menacing hitters in the game, but also to a 13-1 regular-season record and a Super Bowl championship.

It started with the Steelers, arch-rivals who had knocked the Raiders out of the postseason in the last two AFC title games. It started with Atkinson's forearm. And it started with one of the season's more stirring comebacks.

The Raiders trailed Pittsburgh 28-14 with 6:43 left to play. A 10-yard touchdown pass from Ken Stabler to tight end Dave Casper cut the deficit to 28-21 with 2:43 remaining. After failing to move the ball, the

Ted Hendricks (83), "The Mad Stork," stalked opponents with cohorts named "The Destroyer," "The Assassin" and "Dr. Death."

1976 Oakland Raiders

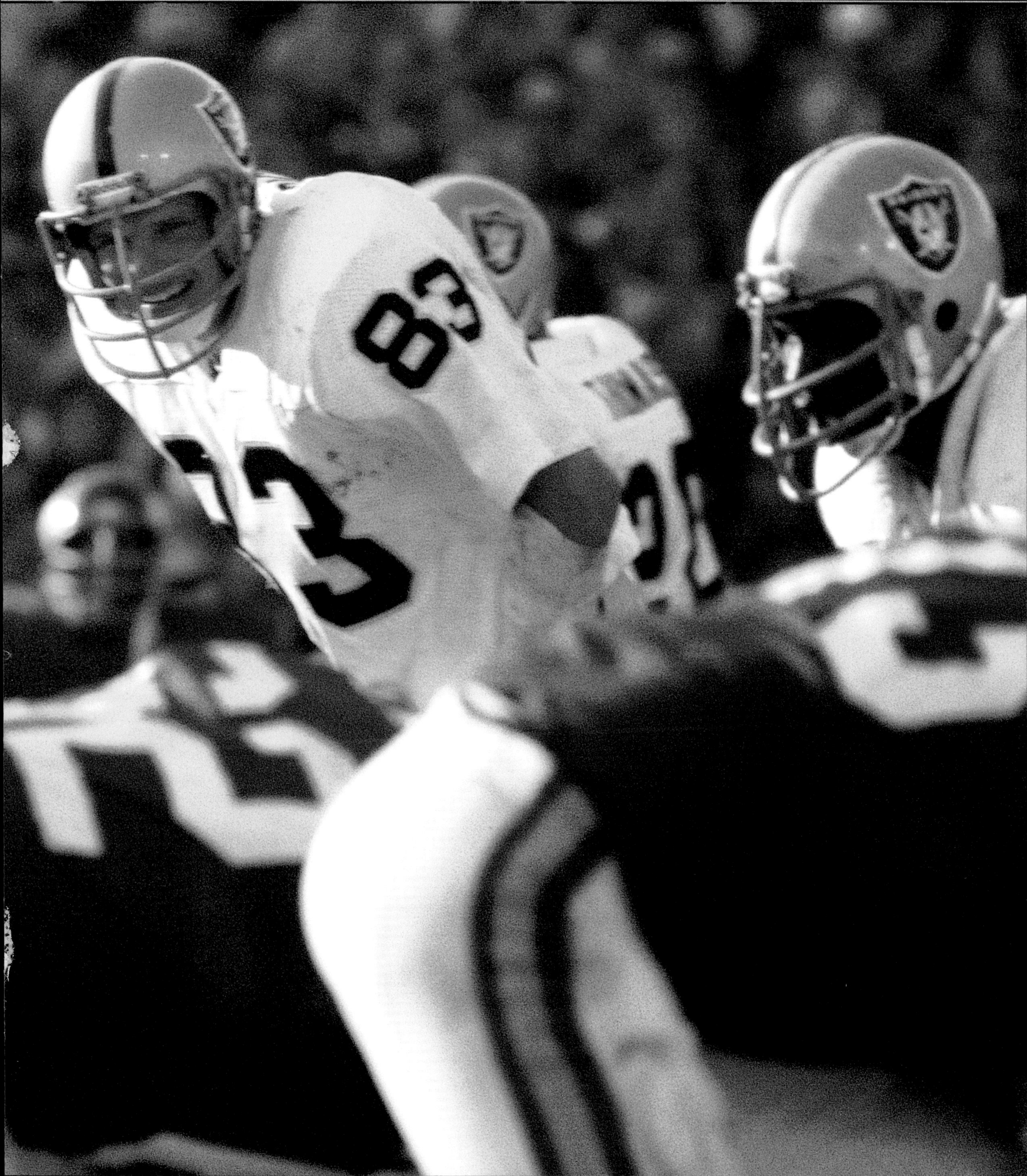

Steelers tried to punt, but Warren Bankston blocked it. On fourth-and-10, Stabler completed a pass to Cliff Branch that carried to the 2-yard line and then Stabler scored himself to tie the game with 1:05 left.

On Pittsburgh's first play after the kickoff, Terry Bradshaw's pass was deflected by Dave Rowe and intercepted by Willie Hall. With 18 seconds on the clock, Fred Steinfort's 21-yard field goal made Oakland a 31-28 winner.

And that tone was set, too. With Stabler throwing to Fred Biletnikoff, one of the best possession receivers in the history of the game, and to Branch, one of the fastest, the '76 Raiders could be down, but never counted out. Stabler completed 22-of-28 passes the next week in a Monday night game against Kansas City, and Oakland won by three points, 24-21. In the third game, the margin was even smaller, 14-13 over Houston.

They beat Denver by a touchdown (17-10) on October 17, the Packers by four points (18-14) on October 24 and the Bears by an extra-point kick (28-27) on November 7.

The close-game magic continued into the playoffs. Against the Patriots in the first round, Oakland started the fourth quarter down 21-10. But with 10 seconds left, Stabler bootlegged the ball into the end zone for a 24-21 win that kept the Raiders playing in the

Ken Stabler, posing with actor James Garner, was called "The Snake" because of his elusive ability.

postseason.

At least seven times that season, they lived on the very edge.

Sometimes, as with Atkinson's hit on Swann, they lived on the very edge of football propriety, too. Or, at least, they wanted other teams to believe they did. The Raiders must have set an NFL record for sinister nicknames, especially on defense. There was "The Assassin," otherwise known as free safety Jack Tatum. There was "The Destroyer," which is how Atkinson was known. There was "Dr. Death," a k a cornerback Skip Thomas.

Of course, "The Mad Stork" played for the Raiders, too, in the person of 6-foot-7 outside linebacker Ted Hendricks. And the list of menacing monikers doesn't include the imposing presence of defensive end John Matuszak, simply known as "Tooz," or defensive tackle Otis Sistrunk, whose bald head and offbeat personality spurred Monday Night Football analyst Alex Karras to suggest that he had played his college football at the University of Mars.

Stabler, too, had a nickname to go with the renegade look of the long hair hanging from the back of his helmet. He was "The Snake," because he so often found ways to slither out of trouble.

For all its big hits and nasty nicknames, the

John Matuszak (72) and George
Atkinson personified the Raiders'
defense: tough and mean.

Raiders' defense didn't dominate the league to the extent that championship teams from other seasons have. Oakland gave up almost 17 points per game, although that average was skewed by New England's seven-touchdown output in a 48-17 Patriots' victory on October 3, the Raiders' only loss. A number of key defenders missed that game, and the

With receivers like Fred Biletnikoff (above), Dave Casper and Cliff Branch, Oakland could always mount a comeback.

next few, with injuries. As a result, Oakland was forced to shift its primary defense to a 3-4 alignment.

That wasn't all bad. The 3-4 allowed Raiders coach John Madden to position Hendricks on the outside, moving Hall into a starting role as an inside linebacker. Hendricks could line up on either end of the defense. Madden allowed him to freelance, and "The Mad Stork" terrorized offenses.

In the AFC Championship Game, a third straight title meeting with Pittsburgh, the Raiders' defense caught a break. Both Franco Harris and Rocky Bleier sat out with injuries, and Oakland won easily, 24-7.

By the time the Raiders played Minnesota in the Super Bowl, the 3-4 defense was peaking. Madden set Tatum, the free safety, on Vikings running back Chuck Foreman; and Foreman, who had gained 1,155 yards and scored 13

touchdowns during the regular season, barely factored in the Super Bowl. He managed only 44 yards on 17 carries and didn't score, although he had five receptions out of the backfield as Minnesota spent most of the day playing catch-up with its passing game.

Oakland led 19-0 in the third quarter and coasted to a 32-14 win.

As the defense evolved during the regular season, the Raiders had to score to ensure their wins. They did. They had triple-threat offensive balance, with fullback Mark van Eeghen's power running (1,012 rushing yards), halfback Clarence Davis's speed (516 yards) and Stabler's polished receiving corps of Casper (53 catches, 691 yards, 10 touchdowns), Branch (46 for 1,111 yards and 12 TDs) and Biletnikoff (43, 551, 7).

Stabler completed 66.7 percent of his passes, the highest percentage for a starting NFL quarterback since Sammy Baugh's 70.3 percent for the 1945 Redskins. He threw for 2,737 yards and 27 touchdowns, with only 17 interceptions.

And, of course, Stabler had that uncanny knack for scoring when he absolutely had to. His most significant heroics came late in the first-round playoff game against the Patriots, the bootleg from the 1-yard line with 10 seconds left that capped a 68-yard drive. That was a second-chance touchdown. When the drive appeared to have stalled on a Stabler incompletion, New England's Ray Hamilton was called for a personal foul for throwing an elbow to Stabler's chin after the pass had been released.

Hamilton chose the wrong time to try to intimidate the Raiders. The first down that came with the penalty saved Oakland's season.

But the story of the '76 Raiders doesn't end with the playoffs and the Super Bowl. It doesn't really end until the summer of 1977 and the denouement of the play that started it all against Pittsburgh back on September 12. The day after that game, Steelers' coach Chuck Noll had referred to a "criminal element" playing in the NFL. There was no doubt he meant Atkinson.

Atkinson filed a slander lawsuit, claiming Noll had tarnished his reputation, and asked

Art Shell was a driving force on the offensive line.

for $2 million in damages. The case went to trial in July. After two weeks of testimony that included video highlights of some of Atkinson's other hits, the jury decided in favor of Noll.

That, though, was Pittsburgh's only victory over the '76 Raiders.

Running back Mark van Eeghen had reason to celebrate after Oakland's Super Bowl win over Minnesota.

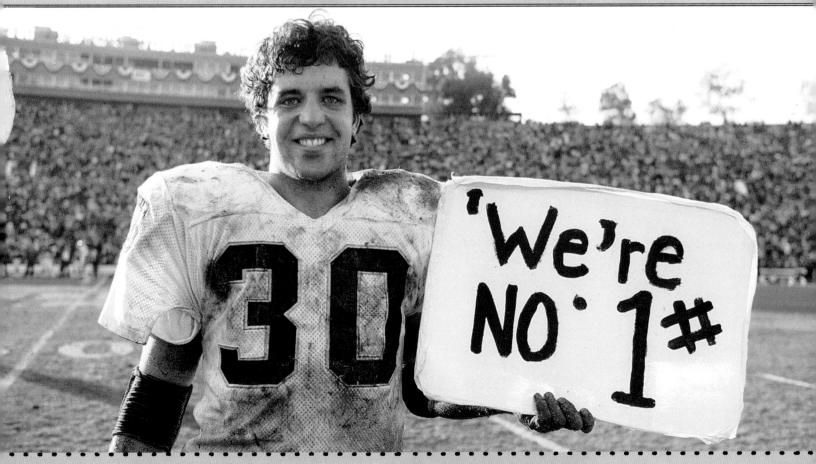

11

It started with their size. They were big, bigger, biggest in the NFL in 1941. John Federovich, a tackle, was 6-foot-5 and 260 pounds. Joe Stydahar, another tackle, stood 6-4 and weighed 230. The two other tackles were 6-3 Lee Artoe and 6-2 Ed Kolman. The guards and ends were huge, too.

They were . . . well, monsters.

As the season wore on, the nickname applied to their talent and their margins of victory, as well. They averaged 36 points per game. They scored 53 against the Cardinals, put 49 up against both the Eagles and the Lions, and tallied 48 against the Cleveland Rams. Those 49 points against Philadelphia all came in the second half, a record for scoring in a half that stood alone for 42 years, until Green Bay matched it against Tampa Bay in 1983.

In their 12 victories, including a pair of postseason games, their average winning margin was 24.8 points. They devoured the opposition, going 10-1 in the regular season before gobbling up Green Bay by 19 points in a divisional playoff game and the Giants by 28 points in the title game.

They were monsters that way, too.

So it began, and so it continues. In every season since then when the Chicago Bears contend, the sobriquet resurfaces. When they're good, they are always the "Monsters of the Midway."

Running back Bill Osmanski runs a sweep around the Giants defense en route to a 37-9 victory in the 1941 championship game. Due to the war effort, only 13,341 fans showed up at Wrigley Field just two weeks after the attack on Pearl Harbor.

1941 Chicago Bears

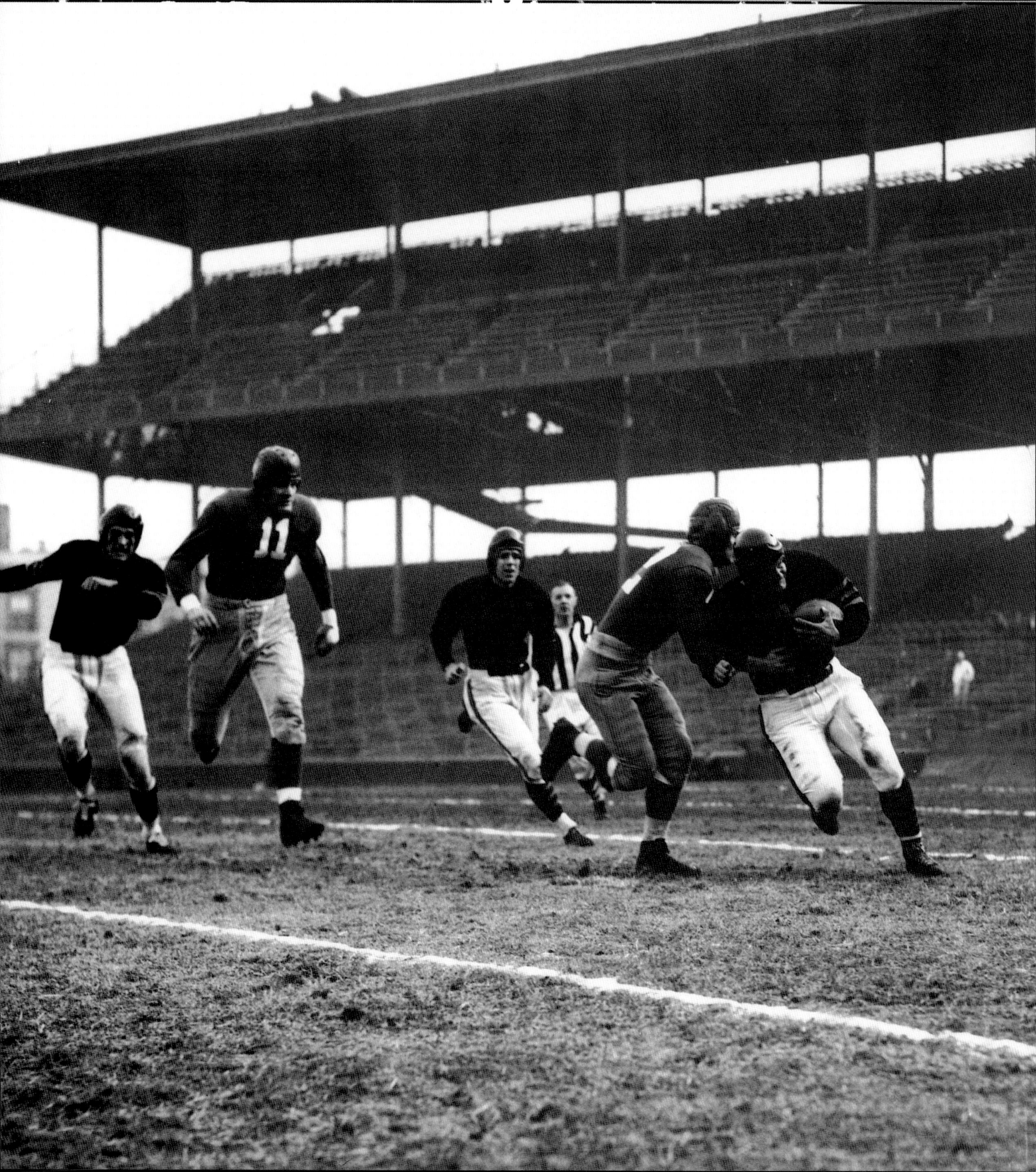

In just his third season, Sid Luckman ran the T to perfection: 1,181 passing yards and nine touchdown throws.

In 1941, they were good. In 1941, the "Monsters" were born. To describe the Bears' dominance that season, the New York press borrowed the phrase from an earlier nickname for the University of Chicago football team. (The New York press apparently wasn't overly familiar with Chicago geography. The '41 Bears played in Wrigley Field, which is nowhere near the Midway.)

A year earlier, Chicago had won the Western Division title with an 8-3 record and then obliterated the Redskins in the NFL title game, 73-0. That set the stage for the "Monsters." By the time the 1941 season ended, Chicago had won those two playoff games, those 10 regular-season games, six preseason games and the annual summer exhibition pitting the defending NFL champs against the College All-Stars. That's 19 wins against one loss.

The one loss? It came by two points to the Packers in the middle of the season. That 16-14 loss was the only game in which the Bears' mighty offense didn't score at least 24 points. But they beat Green Bay in their two other meetings that year, including the divisional playoff.

Chicago's 1941 offense was way ahead of the NFL curve. Owner and coach George Halas had been a believer in the T-formation since the early days of the NFL. He never gave up on it, even as the rest of football stayed stuck in a single-wing or double-wing world. In the late '30s, Halas enlisted the aid of Clark Shaughnessy, a devotee of the T as a college coach, to refine it for the Bears.

In their 1940 championship season, the Bears were the only pro team using the T-formation. In the offseason between 1940 and '41, Eagles coach Earle "Greasy" Neale paid a

Left guard Danny Fortmann (above) and center Clyde "Bulldog" Turner (below) were part of an offensive line that allowed the Bears to lead the league in both passing and rushing.

film company $156 for a copy of the Bears' 73-0 destruction of Washington in the championship game, and used it to learn Halas' T-formation. The first game ever to pit two T-formation pro teams against one another occurred on November 30, 1941, when the Bears visited Philadelphia.

That's the game in which Chicago scored those 49 second-half points. Bears 49, Eagles 14.

Over the next decade, nearly every pro and college team shifted to the T. But in 1941, Halas was the only pro coach fully-utilizing the formation to emphasize speed and deception. His playbook, by one estimate, had as many as 2,300 variations. The Bears put men in motion before the snap. They ran counter plays. They ran double-counter plays. They ran fakes off their double-counter plays.

They baffled defenses.

The Bears had the perfect offensive balance for the T. Sid Luckman, who played tailback in college at Columbia, was the quarterback. In 1941, he was in his third pro season. His best statistical years came later in his career; but in '41, he completed 57.1 percent of his passes for 1,181 yards and nine touchdowns—not bad for a kid still learning a brand new position. Most single-wing offenses started a play with a long snap from center. Halas' T allowed the quarterback to take a direct snap.

In combination with backups Bob Snyder and Young Bussey, each of whom threw for 353 yards, Luckman and the Bears led the league in passing yardage.

Chicago also had the top rushing game in the league. Six different running backs carried the ball at least 36 times that year, a good illustration of the depth on the team and the options the T-formation gave it. George McAfee gained 474 yards and scored six rushing touchdowns. Norm Standlee (414 yards, five TDs), Bill Osmanski (371 yards, four TDs) and Hugh Gallarneau (304 yards, eight

At 6-4 and 230 pounds, tackle Joe Stydahar was typical of the Chicago "Monsters."

TDs) kept defenses guessing.

By late November, the team was being serenaded to the tune of a new fight song called "Bear Down, Chicago Bears," which is still in use today. One of lyricist Al Hoffman's verses credits Halas' unique offense:

George McAfee was the cream of a talented running crop.

We'll never forget the way you thrilled the nation, with your T-formation.

As powerful as the Bears were, they went into the final game of the regular season needing a victory to tie Green Bay for the division title. The Packers had already finished at 10-1. The Bears were 9-1 and facing the crosstown Cardinals in the finale at Comiskey Park. A number of the Packers, including coach Curly Lambeau and future Hall of Fame end Don Hutson, sat in the stands taking notes for a possible playoff.

The date was December 7, 1941.

News of the attack on Pearl Harbor spread through the stands and the clubhouses as the game began. The Cardinals, who had lost to the Bears, 53-7, early in the season, jumped out to a 14-0 lead. Early in the fourth quarter, the Cardinals still led, 24-21. At one juncture, Halas became so incensed he ran onto the field, a violation that cost him a

The Bears had the perfect offensive balance for the T.

fine of $100. At another point, Bears lineman Ray Bray was ejected for punching one of the Cardinals. Meanwhile, the public address system announced to the crowd that all servicemen in attendance were to report immediately to their units.

Ultimately, the Bears won on a 59-yard touchdown pass from Luckman to McAfee, and then a 70-yard touchdown run, again by McAfee. The final score was 34-24.

The playoff with the Packers the next Sunday, and the NFL Championship Game against the Giants on December 21, were played under the cloud of the war effort. Chicago had no trouble with Green Bay, taking a 30-7 lead by halftime and coasting to a 33-14 victory. Against New York, the Bears broke a 9-9 tie midway through the third quarter with three long touchdown drives and took their second straight league title, this time by a 37-9 score.

By then, the public was more concerned with the war than football. Only 13,341 fans showed up at Wrigley Field to watch the championship game. That didn't produce much in the way of gate receipts for the two teams to split.

Each "Monster of the Midway" took home only $430.94 for winning it all.

12

Unitas to Berry. Unitas to Berry. Unitas to Berry. Years after "The Game," Giants middle linebacker Sam Huff said he was still hearing the Yankee Stadium public-address announcer repeat those three little words over and over and over again. They kept rattling around in his head like a bad tune that won't go away.

Twelve times, Johnny Unitas found Raymond Berry with his passes that December 28 afternoon in the 1958 NFL title game. Three of those completions came on the Colts' 66-yard drive to a game-tying field goal with seven seconds left. Two more came on Baltimore's 80-yard touchdown drive in sudden-death overtime as the Colts finally won the championship, 23-17, in what many call the greatest game ever played.

The Giants had the league's best defense in '58, a unit led by Huff and by a ferocious front four of Andy Robustelli, Jim Katcavage, Roosevelt Grier and Dick Modzelewski. Yet, New York couldn't stop Unitas to Berry. Nor, 8:15 into overtime, could the Giants stop Baltimore fullback Alan "The Horse" Ameche from the 1-yard line.

That simple off-tackle play, a 1-yard run, ended it. But the legend of the game, and of the Colts, was just beginning.

So much about that championship defined the '58

Lenny Moore (24) gave the Colts backfield speed and finesse. Alan Ameche was all about power.

1958 Baltimore Colts

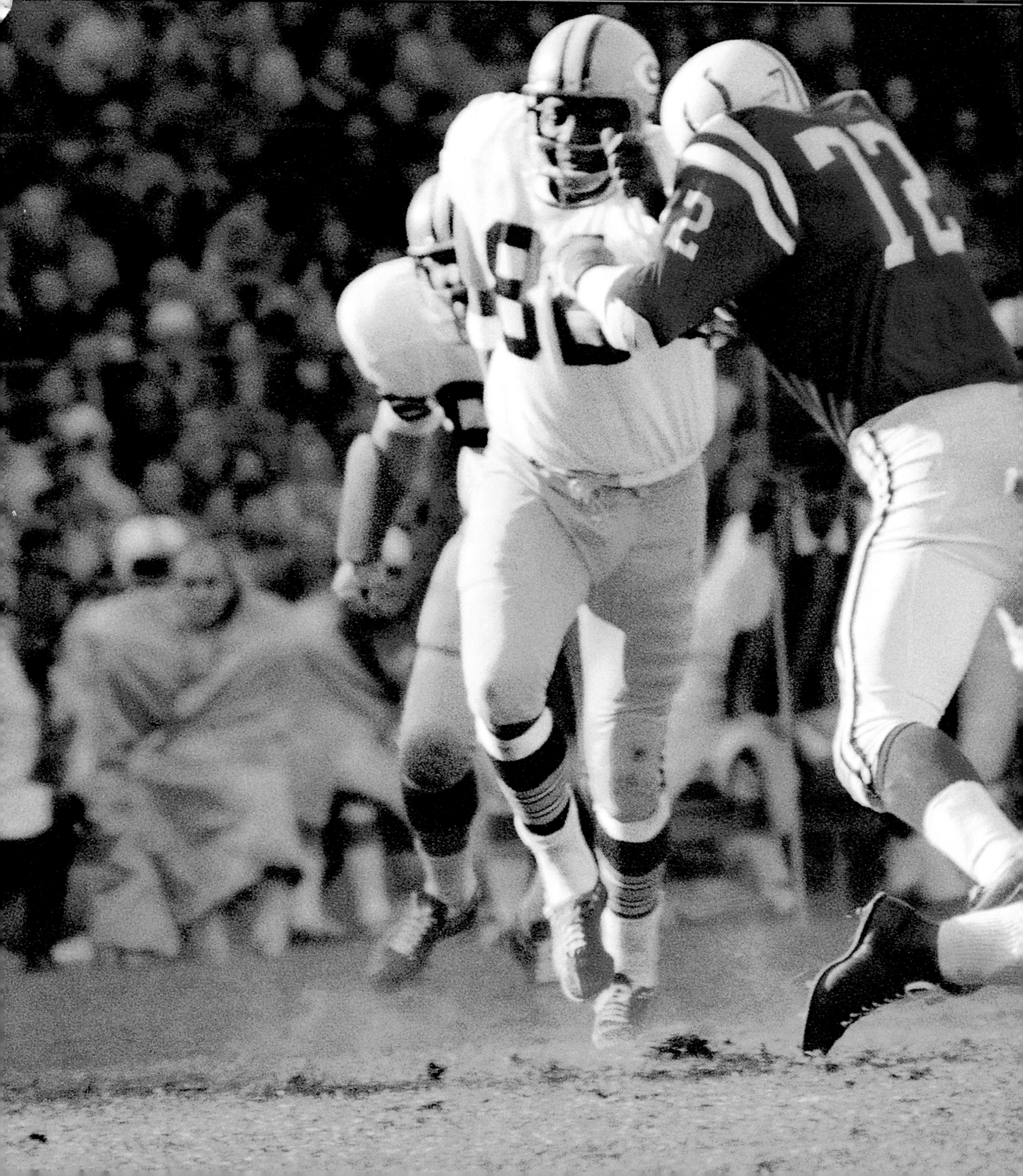

Colts:

• Unitas' two late drives, one at the end of regulation and the other in overtime.

• Berry's 12 receptions for 178 yards, an NFL playoff record that stood for 23 years.

• Steve Myhra's 20-yard field goal that tied the game with seven seconds left.

• Gino Marchetti's game-saving tackle on Frank Gifford that forced a punt and gave Unitas the opportunity for the fourth-quarter drive. Marchetti's leg broke when his team-mate, Gene "Big Daddy" Lipscomb, fell on it assisting with the tackle. Marchetti was carried off the field on a stretcher, but refused to leave the sideline until the game ended.

So much about that game defined pro football, too. Broadcast nationally by NBC, it brought the NFL to the masses in numbers that, for the first time, challenged baseball's long-standing role as America's national pastime. Despite being blacked out in the New York area, the telecast reached an estimated

When everything was on the line, Johnny Unitas (19) was the king of cool.

10.8 million homes and was viewed by nearly 40 million people.

One of those viewers was Texas millionaire Lamar Hunt, who watched the game in Houston and, in the excitement, made a fateful decision to jump head-first into professional football. Two years later, Hunt's American Football League kicked off. Seven years after that, the AFL became a part of the NFL.

Behind Unitas, Berry, Ameche, halfback/receiver Lenny Moore and tackle Jim Parker, the Colts in 1958 featured one of the most electric and potent offenses in the league. Baltimore led the NFL in scoring with an average of nearly 32 points per game. Berry tied for the league lead (with Philadelphia's Pete Retzlaff) in receptions with 56, and Moore caught another 50 passes for 938 yards. Unitas led all quarterbacks in touchdown passes with 19, despite missing two games with injuries. Ameche trailed only Cleveland's Jim Brown in rushing.

Through the '58 season, Unitas was in the midst of his streak of 47 consecutive games with at least one touchdown pass. Included

Go-to receiver Raymond Berry was at his best in the 1958 title game.

was a four-TD performance in Week Two against the Bears.

On defense, Marchetti, Lipscomb and Art Donovan formed an imposing line, while the secondary of Andy Nelson, Ray Brown, Carl Taseff and Milt Davis combined for 27 interceptions.

And yet, the Colts didn't forge their legacy in the fire of the regular season. In fact, they lost three games during the regular season, including their last two. This was not a team on a roll going into postseason play.

The first loss was to the Giants in a game Unitas missed. A week before that November 9 game, he left a 56-0 rout of the Packers with broken ribs and a collapsed lung. Backup George Shaw played in New York, and couldn't engineer a win. The Giants took a 24-21 decision.

Unitas sat out the November 16 game against the Bears, too, but Baltimore's defense handed Chicago its first shutout since 1946. Shaw, Berry, Moore & Co. won, 17-0. That victory, coupled with an earlier 51-38 win over the Bears, proved pivotal because at 9-3, the Colts finished one game

Berry (82) was able to operate because of the blocking of big Jim Parker (below).

ahead of Chicago in the standings.

On November 23, against the Rams in Baltimore, Unitas returned, wearing a protective harness to safeguard his ribs. On his first play, he uncorked a 58-yard touchdown pass to Moore. By the time that 34-7 win ended, he had thrown for 218 yards and a second touchdown. He was back—and so were the Colts.

The following week, the Colts clinched the Western Conference title at home with a 35-27 victory over San Francisco. That was fortuitous, because they closed the season with a pair of games on the West Coast against the Rams and the 49ers, and lost them both. It was deja vu. The previous season, Baltimore had

been tied for the conference lead with Detroit and San Francisco with two games to play and made an identical West Coast swing. The Colts lost twice and finished a game back.

This time, they qualified for the championship game before they went west while New York was battling for the Eastern Conference title. The Giants finished 9-3, tying Cleveland for the lead, and were forced into a December 21 playoff. The Giants were coached by Jim Lee Howell and a couple of young assistants named Tom Landry and Vince Lombardi.

In the divional playoff game, Landry's defense held Jim Brown to 18 rushing yards and shut Cleveland out, 10-0.

But Unitas-to-Berry was a different challenge. No one, including the Giants, was prepared for the precision and tenacity of the Colts' offense in the last two minutes of the championship game's fourth quarter. Down 17-14, Unitas took over on Baltimore's 14-yard line with 1:56 to play. To keep the clock running, New York took away the sideline pass patterns (one of Berry's specialties), so Unitas calmly went over the middle to Moore for 11 yards.

Then, three times in succession, he threw to Berry in the middle of the field. Those three completions gained 62 yards. With seven seconds left, Myhra kicked the tying field goal.

The Giants won the coin toss and had possession first in the overtime. Three plays later, they punted and Baltimore took over on the 20. The key play on the winning drive was a 21-yard completion on third-and-15 to Berry. The Colts reached the 8-yard line, from where they might easily have kicked another field goal for the victory.

But that wasn't Unitas. Instead, he threw another pass, a seven-yard completion to Jim Mutscheller to the 1. Even then, he continued to foil the Giants. Thinking Baltimore would call a play to its left to be in position to kick, New York loaded its defense on that side. Unitas sent Ameche the other way, off-tackle right.

As Ameche lay on the grass in the end zone and the official raised his arms to signal the touchdown, the Colts made their indelible mark in the NFL's ledger-book of brilliance. It was one of football's most inspired performances.

Ameche barrels 1 yard for the championship-winning touchdown against the Giants.

13

S uch a scene! Leon Lett, 290 pounds of beefy defensive tackle, slogging down the Rose Bowl field with Frank Reich's Super Bowl fumble held aloft in taunting triumph, certain to add the insult of another Dallas touchdown to the injury of all those other Cowboys' scores . . . until Buffalo's Don Beebe hurtles in from behind and—horrors!—knocks the ball loose just before Lett reaches the goal line.

Lett's lapse of judgment is only one of the lasting images left by the unforgettable Cowboys of 1992. They also left us souvenir memories of Emmitt Smith breaking loose for big gain after big gain, and of Troy Aikman zipping the ball downfield for yet another acrobatic Michael Irvin reception. They left us the brash confidence of coach Jimmy Johnson, whose favorite phrase, "How 'bout them Cowboys!" echoed through the season, and the rebel bluster of owner Jerry Jones as well.

They certainly left an impression on the Bills, who may never forget the 52-17 tattoo the Cowboys blistered into them in Super Bowl XXVII.

But the image of Lett's glorious moment coming apart amidst the hype and hoopla of the Super Bowl . . . that's the one by which to remember Dallas in '92.

That picture says so much about the Cowboys.

Michael Irvin's brash and cocky style personified the Jimmy Johnson-coached Cowboys.

It says they were young, and embracing youth's exuberance. They were the youngest team in the league, and here they were cavorting through the Super Bowl as if they had not a care in the world. Smith, the league's leading rusher (1,713 yards on 373 carries) and touchdown maker (19), was 23 years old and only in his third pro season. Aikman, the cool quarterback who threw for 3,445 yards and 23 touchdowns and became the Super Bowl MVP, was playing his fourth year and was only 26.

Troy Aikman, who threw for 3,445 yards and 23 touchdowns, was named MVP of the Super Bowl. Emmitt Smith (opposite page) rushed for 1,713 yards and scored 19 touchdowns, leading the league in both categories.

Irvin, the team's best receiver with 78 catches for 1,396 yards and seven touchdowns, had been around for five seasons but sometimes acted as if he'd just turned 18. Kevin Smith, one of the starting cornerbacks, was a rookie.

Lett was all of 24, just finishing his second professional season. His Super Bowl gaffe sprang, perhaps understandably, from the ebullience of his age.

That picture says the Cowboys were proud, too. Johnson wasn't the only member of the organization who exuded confidence. Irvin was a master of the quick-and-cocky quip, on and off the field. Nate Newton, the huge left guard, and right defensive end Charles Haley played and behaved with the aplomb of certain success. Jones, the owner, talked as if his bidding ought to be steering the league. Lett's premature and abortive celebration of a touchdown-that-didn't-happen was hubris, to be sure. But it was in character for the Cowboys, too.

And it says, above all else, that this was a very good football team. It says the Cowboys were so much in command of Buffalo in the Super Bowl that they could absorb a blow such as Lett's lost score and not even blink. As the abashed Lett came back to the sideline, Johnson was laughing. And why not? At halftime, Dallas led the AFC's best team 28-10. By the fourth quarter, the Cowboys had lost the Bills in their rear-view mirror altogether, the same way they put the NFC East Division behind them during the regular season—and the same way they left Philadelphia and San Francisco in their dust in the earlier rounds of the playoffs.

Dallas had

established its place at the top of the NFL's 1992 pecking order early on, when it began the season with a 23-10 victory over the defending Super Bowl-champion Redskins. Washington had rolled through its '91 season and the playoffs, and appeared to be the same powerful and steady machine heading into '92. But when the Redskins opened against Dallas with the no-huddle offense that had been an effective tool for them in Super Bowl XXVI, the Cowboys were lying in wait.

Johnson, expecting the hurry-up attack, had devised a system of signals from the sideline that told his defense where to line up, undoing the advantage Washington hoped to gain with the no-huddle. At the end of the first quarter, the Redskins had a total offense of minus-2, and they finished with only 264 yards. The Cowboys sacked quarterback Mark Rypien twice, including an 11-yard loss on a blitz by linebacker Vinson Smith on the first play from scrimmage. Rypien had been sacked only seven times the previous season.

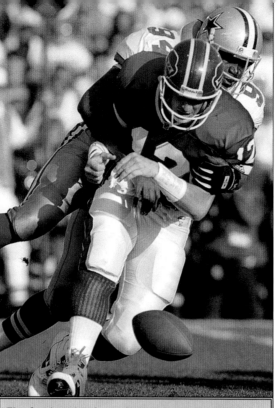

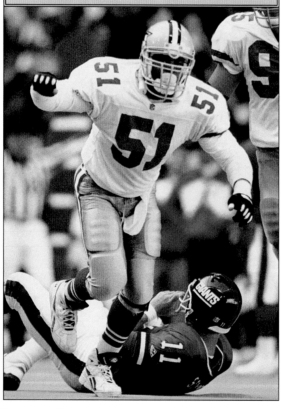

The Cowboys' defense featured end Charles Haley (94) and linebacker Ken Norton Jr. (51 below).

Smith, meanwhile, gained 139 yards on 26 carries and Aikman passed for 216 yards, sounding tones that would be heard throughout the league as the year continued.

The following week, Dallas built a 34-0 lead over the Giants and held off a furious New York comeback to win 34-28. The season was two weeks old, and two old NFC East nemeses had already been dispatched.

In 1989, the Cowboys had been the NFL's bottom-feeders with a 1-15 record. In a very short three-year turnaround, they'd become America's Team II, the second coming of the Dallas dynasty that had appeared in five Super Bowls, winning two, during the decade of the '70s.

Jones and Johnson did the rebuilding. Smith, Aikman and Irvin did the scoring. Smith, in particular, was the "main man" in Dallas in '92. His 1,713 yards on the ground accounted for 80.1 percent of the Cowboys' rushing offense. Dallas's second-leading rusher was Curvin Richards, who gained 176 yards on 49 carries before he was unceremoniously cut by

Johnson because of two second-half fumbles during a late-season game. When Aikman handed the ball to a back, the back who took it almost invariably was Smith.

During one stretch, Smith went over the 100-yard mark in five straight games. He gained 174 yards on the ground against Atlanta, 163 against the Eagles, 152 against the Raiders and 139 against the Redskins in the opener. In Dallas's three playoff victories, including the Super Bowl, Smith picked up 114 yards (Philadelphia in the divisional round), 114 yards again (San Francisco in the NFC Championship Game) and 108 (Buffalo).

In addition, his 59 receptions out of the backfield were the most by any NFC running back, and his 2,048 total yards from scrimmage were second in the NFL to the Bills' Thomas.

On December 13, the Cowboys dropped their third and last game of the year by a 20-17 score to the Redskins when a controversial Aikman fumble was recovered in the end zone by Washington's Danny Copeland in the closing minutes. It cost Dallas home-field advantage in the NFC Championship Game. After a no-sweat 34-10 victory over the Eagles at home in the divisional playoff round, the Cowboys traveled to San Francisco to meet the 14-2 49ers. On a sloppy, shredded Candlestick Park field, Aikman completed two long passes to Alvin Harper that set up touchdowns, and Dallas won 30-20.

The Super Bowl was a laugher, helped in no small measure by Buffalo's ineptitude. Quarterbacks Jim Kelly and Reich, who replaced Kelly in the second quarter after a hit by Dallas linebacker Ken Norton Jr., threw four interceptions. The Cowboys sacked them four times.

And the Bills fumbled eight times, losing five of them. Thirty-five of Dallas's 52 points came as a result of those nine turnovers.

And it could have been worse.

Lett could have scored.

Leon Lett's Super Bowl ramble ended in frustration, but the cocky Cowboys still overpowered the Bills.

14

I n 1975, the Pittsburgh Steelers were following one very tough act. Their own.

The Steelers in 1974 had set a high standard for football the throwback way: a muscle-up running game and a defense that took no prisoners. Later in the decade, they would win a pair of Super Bowls ('78 and '79) with a style that was, by comparison, wide-open. But in '74, Pittsburgh won Super Bowl IX over Minnesota by playing good old-fashioned, snot-rockin' tackle football.

Against the Vikings, Franco Harris sledge-hammered his way to 158 yards and the "Steel Curtain" defense played as well as a defense can play. Minnesota gained only 17 yards on the ground and 119 yards in total offense.

So the Steelers' 1975 season opened with a challenge to themselves: Top that!

They did. They improved on a world championship.

The 1975 Steelers scored more points (373 in 1975, 305 in '74), gave up fewer points (162 vs. 189) and won more games (12-2 in the regular season, compared to 10-3-1 in '74) than their Super Bowl-champion team of the year before.

There were obvious reasons for the improvement,

Lynn Swann's Super Bowl X acrobatics included a spectacular catch (right) over Cowboys defender Mark Washington.

including the maturation of one of the best draft classes the NFL has ever seen. In '74, the Steelers had drafted Lynn Swann, Jack Lambert, John Stallworth and Mike Webster, among others. In '75, all four of those future Hall of Famers moved into primary roles. Swann and Stallworth replaced Ron Shanklin and Frank Lewis as the starting wide receivers. Lambert became the leader of the defense. Webster shared time at center with veteran Ray Mansfield, and was starting by the end of the year.

Mostly, though, Pittsburgh was stronger in 1975 because the "Steel Curtain" just became . . . well, steelier. Mean Joe Greene, Ernie Holmes, L.C. Greenwood, Dwight White, Jack Ham, Andy Russell, Mel Blount, Lambert . . . it may not have seemed possible to the poor Vikings, but the defense that cold-cocked them in '74 hit even harder and made even bigger plays in 1975.

When games were on the line, the "Steel

Behind a rock-solid defensive front loomed one of the fiercest middle linebackers in the game—Jack Lambert.

Curtain" slammed down with vehemence. Usually, that vehemence took the form of sacks, of forced fumbles, of interceptions and of noggin-numbing tackles. A sample:

• Against the Bengals in an AFC Central Division showdown in December, Lambert crunched Cincinnati's Boobie Clark with a hit that knocked the ball loose. Lambert picked it up, ran 21 yards with it and then pitched to cornerback J.T. Thomas, who went another 21 yards for a touchdown. The Steelers won 35-14 to clinch the division title.

• Against the Colts in a first-round playoff game, Ham blasted Baltimore quarterback Bert Jones on a sack near the goal line and forced a fumble. Russell picked up the loose ball and tramped 93 yards for a touchdown. Pittsburgh won 28-10.

• Against the Raiders in the AFC Championship Game, Lambert recovered three fumbles as the Steelers forced five Oakland turnovers on the frigid, icy Three Rivers Stadium artificial turf. The defense had to be good in that game. The Steelers turned the ball over eight times themselves. Pittsburgh won,

The imposing pair of Joe Greene (75) and Ernie Holmes (below) manned the interior of the Steelers' "Stunt 43" defensive alignment.

16-10.

• In the Super Bowl, Greenwood and White turned Cowboys quarterback Roger Staubach into a human tackling dummy. Staubach was sacked a Super Bowl-record seven times. Three of his passes were intercepted, one on the last play of the game with Dallas threatening to score the winning touchdown. Strong safety Mike Wagner batted the ball into the air and free safety Glen Edwards came down with it in the end zone, preserving Pittsburgh's 21-17 victory.

The Steelers recorded 43 sacks during the regular season, Holmes leading the way with $8^1/_2$. They picked off 27 passes. Blount led the league with 11 interceptions, including at least one in six straight games.

Holmes and Mean Joe Greene made for the most imposing and intimidating pair of interior linemen in football. In Pittsburgh's "Stunt 43" alignment, those two set the offensive center in their sights, one on each side, and angled in toward the poor snapper. The pressure those two put on the middle of an offense launched the Steel Curtain's

The run-pass tandom of Franco Harris (above) and Terry Bradshaw (below) carved up opposing defenses.

complex stunts and power pass rushes. In only two games did the defense allow a running back any meaningful room to move. Against Buffalo on September 28, O.J. Simpson gained 227 yards on 28 carries. Simpson scored only one touchdown, but the Bills won, 30-21. O.J. was at the very peak of his career in the mid-'70s. He gained 2,003 yards in 1973 and was on his way to a league-leading 1,817 yards in '75.

Three weeks later, the Bears' Mike Adamle gained 110 yards and Roland Harper, his backfield mate, picked up another 86. But neither reached the end zone and Chicago didn't back up its ground game with anything else. The "Steel Curtain" kept quarterback Gary Huff to 46 passing yards on an 8-for-22 day. The final score was Pittsburgh 34, Chicago 3.

Meanwhile, Harris, Swann, Stallworth, Rocky Bleier and quarterback Terry Bradshaw made the Steelers' offense go. Harris' 1,246 rushing yards were second—albeit a distant second—in the league to Simpson and Bleier added 528 yards on the ground. Bradshaw threw for 2,055 yards and 18 touchdowns, with only nine interceptions. Swann led the AFC with 11 TD receptions.

After the loss at home to Buffalo in the second week of the season, the Steelers won 11 straight games. Going into the last week, they'd won 10 straight road games, too, dating back to 1974. But, the division title already clinched, they stumbled in Los Angeles against the Rams, losing 10-3.

The Rams were even stingier than the Steelers that year on defense, allowing just 135 points (9.6 per game). But in the NFC Championship Game, Dallas stunned L.A., 37-7, with Staubach throwing four touchdown passes, including three to Preston Pearson. That set up a classic Cowboys-Steelers Super Bowl—Staubach throwing his fancy passing game into the teeth of Pittsburgh's "Steel Curtain." It was new-school football vs. old-school football.

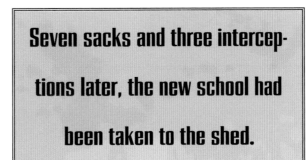

Seven sacks and three interceptions later, the new school had been taken to the shed.

Seven sacks and three interceptions later, the new school had been taken to the shed. Bradshaw and Swann, not Staubach and Pearson, were the glittery passing combination in the Super Bowl. Swann snagged a crucial 32-yard pass on the sideline, made a leaping catch over the Cowboys' Mel Renfro for 53 yards and scored the Steelers' last touchdown on a 64-yard bomb. His four receptions for 161 yards won him the vote as the most valuable player.

Still, Steelers coach Chuck Noll knew what had taken Pittsburgh that far. With less than two minutes to play and Pittsburgh facing a fourth-and-nine situation at the Dallas 41-yard line, Noll eschewed the risk of a blocked kick or a bad snap on a punt. Instead, he ran Bleier into the line on fourth down. The gain was only 2 yards, so the Cowboys took over. Noll obviously had faith that his defense could stop one final drive, regardless of field position.

The "Steel Curtain" rewarded that faith. When Edwards intercepted Staubach as the gun sounded, the Steelers had won, 21-17. Their 1975 act had outdone their '74 exploits.

In a classic Super Bowl matchup, the old-school defense prevailed over the new-school offense.

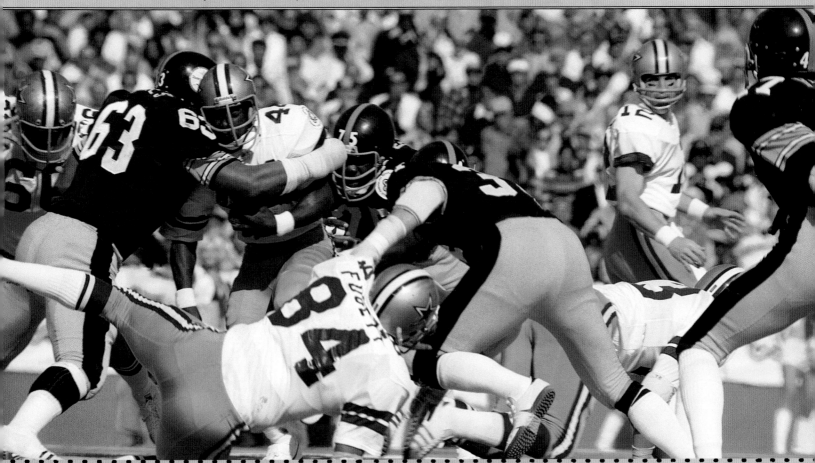

15

T

wo games leapt off the page at the 49ers when the NFL committed its 1994 schedule to paper.

At Kansas City on September 11.

At home against Dallas on November 13.

The other 14 games? They were important, to be sure. San Francisco had won four Super Bowls and been in the thick of nearly every postseason for a decade and a half because it took every game seriously, not just one here and one there. But by a wide margin, nothing else on the '94 schedule loomed as large for the 49ers as Kansas City in September and Dallas in November. Couldn't possibly.

When they played Kansas City, the 49ers faced a legend of their own making. Joe Montana, who had taken San Francisco to those four Super Bowl victories during his tenure in the Bay Area, was quarterbacking the Chiefs. A victory over Montana would validate the decision to trade him and install Steve Young as the starter.

And when they played Dallas, the 49ers faced their own personal nemesis. The Cowboys had won the last two Super Bowls. For two years running, they'd beaten San Francisco in the NFC Championship Game, stopping the 49ers one game short of their goal. Somehow, San Francisco had to find a way past the Dallas bugaboo. The November 13 game was the chance to make a statement.

The 49ers weren't going to need more offense to beat either of those teams. They already had the best in the league, and it hadn't taken them to the Super Bowl. In 1993, San Francisco had led the league in points scored and total offense, and yet lost to the Cowboys

Ricky Watters (32) and the 49ers ran roughshod over the Cowboys in a payback NFC title game.

38-21 in the NFC title game.

So if the 49ers were going to make a difference in '94, they were going to have to do it with defense.

They did. By the time owner Eddie DeBartolo, general manager Carmen Policy and coach George Seifert were through tinkering, seven new defensive starters were in place. And the new-comers weren't jour-neymen. They were defi-nite upgrades, stars brought in piecemeal as free agents or through crafty trades.

Defensive end Richard Dent, one of the standouts on the Bears' renowned "46" defense, joined up. So did linebackers Rickey Jackson, Gary Plummer and Ken Norton Jr., who came over from Dallas, of all teams. Toi Cook, a defensive back, was new. In the second half of the season, defensive end Tim Harris, a sack special-ist, signed on.

And, of course, there was Deion.

As in Neon Deion. As in "Prime Time."

Occasionally known as Deion Sanders, all-galaxy cornerback.

Sanders wasn't there in the 49ers' opener, a 44-14 win over the Raiders. Nor was he there on September 11 against the Chiefs, who—at least temporarily—had made San Francisco's brain-trust rue the deal that had banished Montana after the '92 season. Montana's two touchdown passes sent Kansas City to a 24-17 victory, and sent the 49ers home wonder-ing what they'd been thinking when they gave up on him. Young passed for 288 yards and one touchdown that day, but he also threw two intercep-tions and did nothing to change a percep-tion that he had diffi-culty winning the big games.

The loss to the Chiefs was a blow to a proud organization.

Could Sanders, who signed a con-tract the next week, have changed the outcome? Perhaps not. The 49ers were without two of their starting offensive linemen, which paved the way for Chiefs linebacker Derrick Thomas and defensive end Neil Smith to hound Young all afternoon. Plus, Dent went down with an injured knee in the fourth quarter. The odds were against a Young tour de force, with or without Neon Deion.

The '94 season was prime time for Deion Sanders.

But once Sanders began to play, the 49ers began to play better—a lot better. His first action came in the third week of the season, a 34-19 victory over the Rams in which he played only in nickel formations. The following week, he sealed a 24-13 win over the Saints with a 74-yard touchdown on an interception return of a Jim Everett pass—and the

man coverage and the 49ers won in another laugher, 50-14.

And against San Diego in a December game, he picked off a Stan Humphries pass and went 90 yards with it for his third long touchdown return of the season. The 49ers jumped out to a 31-9 lead and coasted in, 38-15.

Sanders' stifling work at cornerback gave

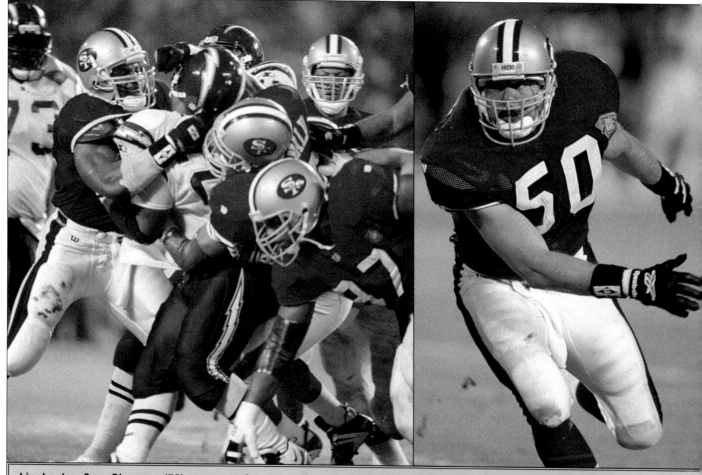

Linebacker Gary Plummer (50) was one of seven starters the 49ers acquired to strengthen their defense.

show was on.

The rest of San Francisco's season was played in "Prime Time." Against Atlanta, a 42-3 rout, Sanders returned an interception for 93 yards and a touchdown. Against the Rams, a 31-27 squeaker, he deflected a last-gasp pass from Chris Miller to Flipper Anderson in the end zone, saving the day for San Francisco. Against the Falcons in the rematch, he smothered wide receiver Andre Rison with man-to-

the rest of the defense the freedom to play much more aggressively. As the season wore on, Seifert called fewer zone coverages and more blitzes than ever before.

And the 49ers went on a 10-game winning streak.

One of those wins occurred November 13. The 21-14 victory over the Cowboys was a tribute to the strides made by the defense. San Francisco intercepted three Troy Aikman

The 49ers' offense had plenty of speed, with Watters (above) carrying the ball out of the backfield and Jerry Rice at wide receiver.

passes, two of which came near the goal line as Dallas appeared ready to score. Merton Hanks, who had moved from cornerback to free safety to make room in the lineup for Sanders, picked off those two. In the first quarter, the Cowboys ran only one play beyond the 50-yard line; in the third period, they didn't cross it at all.

Now the Niners knew they could handle the champs.

Now, too, they knew Young could handle the high-pressure games. Despite the fact that his name wasn't Joe Montana, Young took San Francisco's West Coast offense to unprecedented heights in '94. The 49ers scored 505 points, an average of 31.5 per game, the fourth-highest total in NFL history. Young passed for 3,969 yards and 35 touchdowns (against only 10 interceptions), compiling a league-record completion percentage of 70.3 and a quarterback efficiency rating of 112.8. The player who had held the efficiency rating record he broke was Montana.

When the playoffs began, the offense and the defense both were peaking. Chicago put up little resistance in the divisional round. After an early fumble, the 49ers scored on six straight possessions and won 44-15.

Then came—who else?—the Cowboys. In the NFC Championship Game. Again.

As it did in the November game, the defense won the day. In the game's first five minutes, San Francisco forced turnovers the first three times Dallas had the ball, and the 49ers turned all three into touchdowns. The first score came on a 44-yard interception return by Eric Davis, the other cornerback, as the Cowboys tried to steer clear of Sanders. Young threw two touchdown passes, and San Francisco was a 38-28 winner.

After that emotional win, Super Bowl XXIX might just as well have been one of those "other" 14 regular-season games for the 49ers. In fact, it was a rematch of one of them. San

Diego, a 38-15 loser to San Francisco in December, emerged from the AFC playoffs to meet the Niners in the Super Bowl.

Nothin' to it. Young moved the offense at will. San Francisco scored on three plays to start the game and on four plays the next time it had the ball. The fourth possession, another touchdown. The fifth, same result.

When the onslaught ended, Young had thrown a Super Bowl-record six touchdown passes—breaking, of course, another Montana mark—and the Niners were 49-26 winners.

It was closure, both for Young, who established himself as the new standard for quarterbacks in San Francisco, and for the 49ers, who reinstalled themselves as the team to beat in the NFL.

Steve Young compiled an incredible quarterback rating of 112.8, breaking the record set by Joe Montana.

16

On game day, it rained. The night before the game, it rained. The day before the game, it rained. By the time the Philadelphia Eagles and the Los Angeles Rams kicked off in the 1949 NFL Championship Game, more than three inches of rain had fallen at the L.A. Coliseum. The field was a quagmire.

For the Eagles, the conditions seemed perfect. The team was built for mud. It had the top power running offense in the league with halfback Steve Van Buren, who was big, fast and sure-footed. Van Buren led the league in rushing in 1949 with 1,146 yards and 11 touchdowns, as Philadelphia brought the league's highest-scoring team into the championship matchup. The Eagles were prepared to handle the swamp-like turf.

Los Angeles, however, needed successful passing from quarterback Bob Waterfield to succeed. The soaked Coliseum field was bad news for the Rams, who had never played a home game in the rain since moving to Los Angeles from Cleveland in 1946. And not surprisingly, the game played to form.

In the muck and the mud, Waterfield and his backup, Norm Van Brocklin, completed only 10 passes between them for a paltry 98 yards. End Tom Fears, who led the league in receptions with 77, wasn't a factor and Philadelphia won, 14-0, to capture its second consecutive championship.

Eagles' halfback Frank Reagan intercepts a pass by the Rams' Bob Waterfield during the muddy 1949 NFL Championship Game.

1949 Philadelphia Eagles

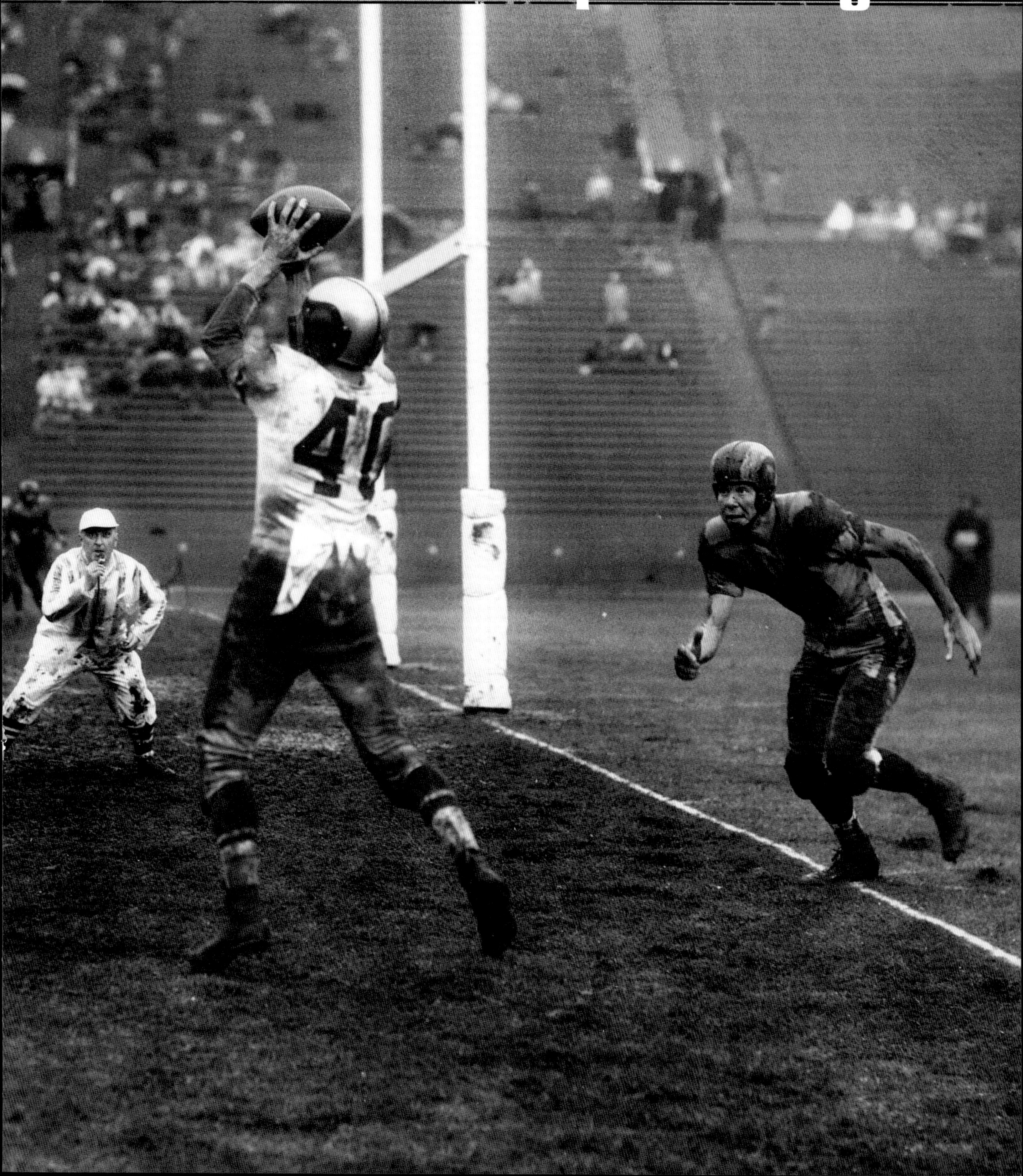

Despite their obvious advantage, the last thing the Eagles wanted to do as they awoke in southern California that rainy December 18 morning was play football. In fact, they petitioned NFL commissioner Bert Bell to postpone the game, to wait a week and play on Christmas Day when the weather was likely to be improved. With better weather, the game would attract a larger crowd. That was important, because the size of the players' checks for the championship game was tied to the size of the turnout.

Bell denied the request and the game went on as scheduled, partly because it was to be broadcast nationally on radio. Nobody wanted to play, and very few wanted to watch. A crowd of 70,000 to 90,000 had been expected. Instead, only 22,245 braved the monsoon.

Perhaps the Eagles should be excused for a little petulance over the playing conditions. This was their second championship game in as many seasons and on both occasions weather cost them a bigger payday. In 1948, Philadelphia met the Chicago Cardinals for the NFL title on December 19 in Philly's Shibe Park, and the game

Tommy Thompson was one of several quarterbacks who enjoyed early success passing out of the T-formation.

was played in a driving blizzard. Only 28,864 turned out then.

Van Buren, in particular, was infuriated by Bell's 1949 decision. A year earlier, he nearly missed the Eagles' 7-0 title-game victory (in which he scored the only touchdown) because he assumed the game would not be played when he woke up in his suburban Philly home and saw the snowstorm. Only a frantic phone call from coach Earle "Greasy" Neale got the star running back to the park on time.

In L.A., Van Buren apparently re-directed his anger from Bell to the Rams. Playing in a

rage, he plowed through the slop and the L.A. defense for 196 yards on 31 carries. The yardage was an NFL championship-game record. He didn't score, but his bruising, ball-control runs kept Waterfield, Fears and the Rams' offense off the field.

Not that Philadelphia's defense really needed the help. Neale's famous "Eagle Defense" was in its prime in 1949. The Eagles' coach had come up with the 5-2-4 alignment in 1947 to counter the league's new wave of passing attacks. In the late '40s, quarterbacks such as the Redskins' Sammy Baugh, the Bears' Sid Luckman, the

---

The Eagles had future Hall of Famers on offense (Steve Van Buren, below) and defense (Chuck Bednarik, above).

Defensive end Pete Pihos exhausted the Rams' offense—and defense—during the championship game.

Rams' Waterfield and Philadelphia's own Tommy Thompson were enjoying unprecedented success with the forward pass out of the T-formation popularized in the early part of the decade by Luckman and Bears owner/coach George Halas.

Neale's innovative defensive formation was the best rebuttal. As the defense lined up, seven players took positions on the line, but the ends could drop back into pass coverage and defend a play much as outside linebackers do today. (The Eagle Defense is considered the father of the modern era's 3-4 defensive alignment; some have credited it as the source for Buddy Ryan's stunningly-successful "46" defense with the 1985 Bears.) It was also the first defense to use, in effect, two cornerbacks and two safeties rather than four defensive halfbacks.

In the 1950s, the Eagle Defense became the alignment of choice in the NFL. In 1949, nobody played it better than the team that originated it. Hall of Famer Alex Wojciechowicz starred at one of the linebacker spots, and the secondary featured Russ Craft, Neill Armstrong, Pat McHugh and Frank Reagan.

The line of Vic Sears, Mike Jarmoluk, Frank "Bucko" Kilroy, Pete Pihos and Jay MacDowell dominated in the trenches and made life particularly miserable for Waterfield in the rainy championship game.

The 1949 Eagles also had a rookie who saw plenty of playing time on both offense and defense. Philadelphia's top draft choice was future Hall of Famer Chuck Bednarik, a center and linebacker who in 1960 was the last man in the NFL still playing on both sides of the ball full-time.

The Eagles' defense gave up the fewest points in the league in 1949 (an average of 11 per game), and also allowed the fewest total yards (236 per game) and the fewest passing yards (134 per game). In the inclement weather on December 18, the polished Rams passing attack didn't have a chance. L.A.'s running game didn't work, either. It netted only 21 rushing yards, which at the time was the lowest total in NFL playoff history.

Philadelphia opened the '49 season with a 7-0 win in the Polo Grounds against the New York Bulldogs. The Eagles were 3-0 when they traveled to Chicago to meet the Bears on October 16. That was their only loss, a 38-21 decision.

The rest of the way, they weren't challenged. They beat Baugh's Redskins by 35 points the next week, and later walloped the Bulldogs in a rematch of the opener, 42-0. After the loss to the Bears, their margin of victory was more than 20 points in six of their remaining eight games.

That included a home game against the Rams on November 6. Final score: Eagles 38, Los Angeles 14. When the regular season ended, Philadelphia had won the Eastern Conference with an 11-1 record. The Steelers were second, with a distant 6-5-1 mark.

So the Eagles were favored in the championship game, with or without the rain. Early in the second period in the waterlogged Coliseum, Thompson caught the Rams focusing on Van Buren and threw three quick completions, the first two to end Jack Ferrante. From the 31-yard line, the third completion went to Pete Pihos, who snagged the ball at the 15 and crossed the goal line untouched.

Philadelphia scored again in the third quarter when defensive end Leo Skladany blocked a Waterfield punt, recovered the ball and rolled into the end zone from the 2-yard line. Against the Eagle Defense, the Rams didn't advance beyond Philadelphia's 25-yard line.

The Eagles, then, became the only team in NFL history to record shutouts in consecutive championship games, first in the snow in 1948 and then in the rain in '49.

They just didn't get rich doing it.

> In the inclement weather on December 18, the polished Rams passing attack didn't have a chance.

Jack Ferrante (left) was a pass-catching threat and Vic Sears (right) was a fixture in the trenches.

17

The Kansas City Chiefs of 1969 may have been the least likely juggernaut in the history of professional football. And yet, there they were on January 11, 1970, dominating the mighty Minnesota Vikings in Super Bowl IV on a cool, misty southern afternoon at Tulane Stadium in New Orleans.

Make no mistake. The Chiefs were strong. Their 23-7 victory over the Vikings wasn't a fluke. They brought one of the best defenses of all time into the Super Bowl, along with Len Dawson, a smart, gutty quarterback, and Hank Stram, an innovative head coach whose tactics were ahead of their time. When Kansas City whipped Minnesota in Super Bowl IV, the Chiefs became worthy champions of professional football.

But they weren't the champions of the AFL Western Division. At 11-3, they finished a game-and-a-half behind the 12-1-1 Oakland Raiders. In any earlier Super Bowl year, that would have left them out of the postseason picture. But the Chiefs were allowed to keep playing by virtue of a one-year quirk in scheduling. In 1969, the last year the NFL and AFL operated as separate entities, the 10-team AFL decided to add an extra tier of playoff games to its postseason schedule, allowing the second-place teams in the Eastern and Western divisions to gain new life.

Under the one-year format, the No. 2 team in the

Middle linebacker Willie Lanier (63) was one big reason why the Chiefs led the league in every major defensive category.

1969 Kansas City Chiefs

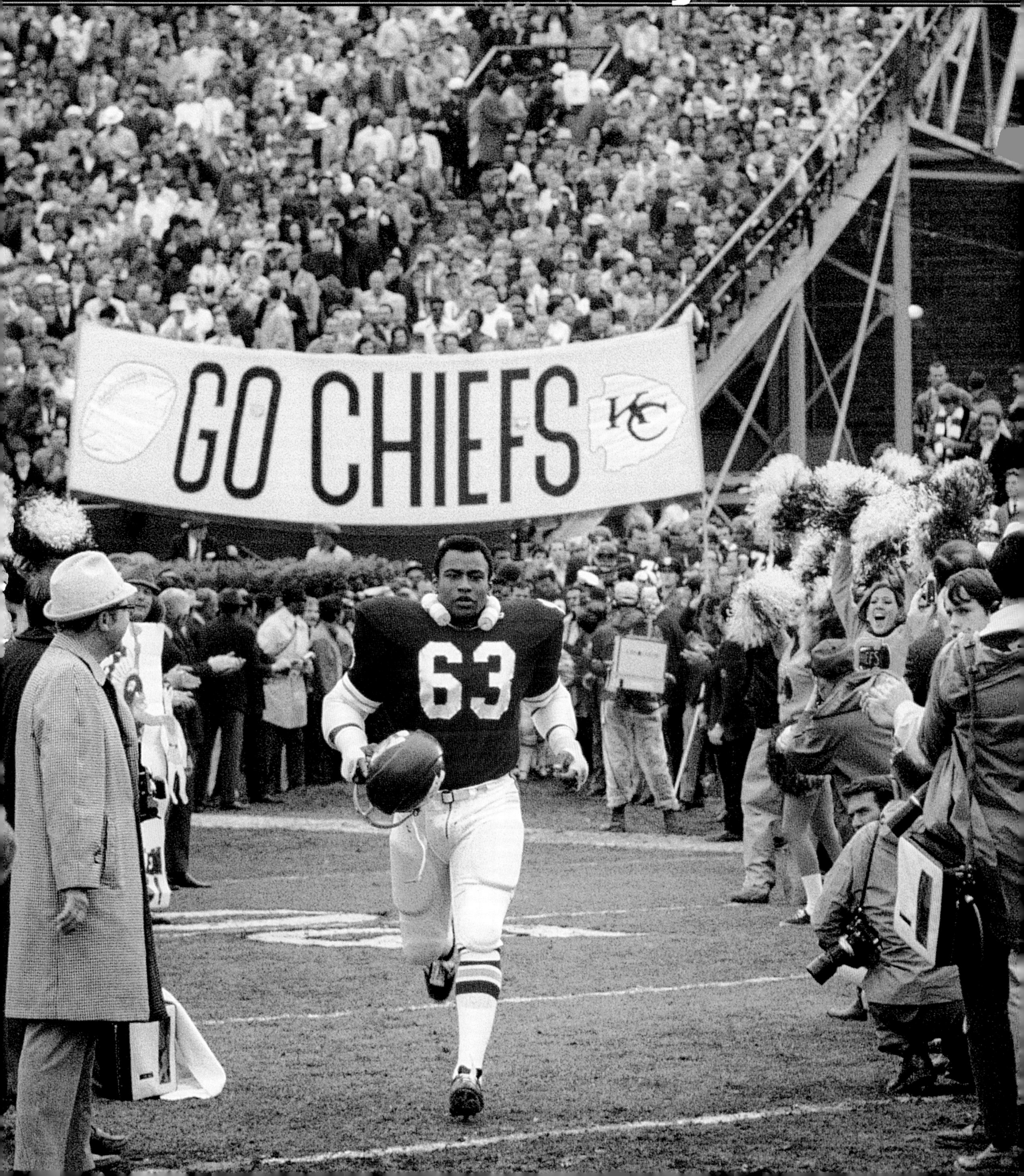

Eastern Division played the No. 1 team in the Western Division—and vice-versa. Then the first-round winners met in a championship game to determine the AFL's representative in the Super Bowl. It was an early preview of today's wild-card playoff system—an unusual format that would not reappear for many years.

Kansas City's second-place finish wasn't the only reason it didn't appear destined to be a team for the ages. During the year's second game, Dawson injured his knee in a 31-0 victory over the Patriots and didn't play again for six weeks. When he returned, he was less than spectacular. Dawson completed 59 percent of his 1969 passes, but his touchdown-to-interception ratio was a modest 9-to-13—hardly the stuff of greatness.

Even worse, the quarterback who replaced him in Boston, Jacky Lee, broke an ankle against Cincinnati the next week. That meant the Chiefs played a significant chunk of their 14 regular-season games with a third-string quarterback who until then had never thrown a pass in professional football.

Fortunately, Mike Livingston was up to the task. He passed for 1,123 yards and four touchdowns while throwing only six interceptions—enough to keep the team afloat.

After a 24-19 loss to the Bengals in their third game, the Chiefs even began a seven-game winning streak. Livingston kept the team on an even keel during the streak before yielding to Dawson in the second half of a November 2 game at Buffalo—a 29-7 victory.

Kansas City's image as a team of excellence was tarnished further during Super Bowl week. Five days before the game, national news reports named Dawson as the subject of a federal subpoena in a Justice Department investigation of a Detroit gambler. The Kansas City quarterback subsequently was cleared of any wrongdoing, but the story smeared his reputation and distracted the championship-minded Chiefs.

Any uneasiness over Kansas City's offense

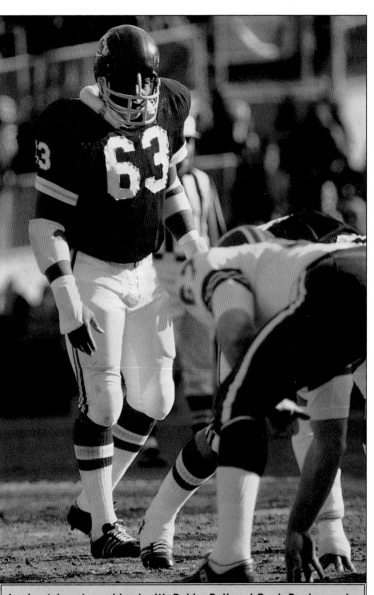

Lanier (above) combined with Bobby Bell and Buck Buchanan to give the defense a Hall of Fame look.

was more than balanced by its outstanding defense. When the regular season ended, the Chiefs led their league in every major defensive statistical category: points allowed (12.6 per game), rushing yards allowed (77.9), passing yards allowed (177.9) and first downs allowed (12.9). Kansas City also led the AFL in interceptions (32) and sacks (48).

Three future Hall of Fame defenders led the way: outside linebacker Bobby Bell, middle linebacker Willie Lanier and tackle Buck

Bell (above) was a defensive force while Len Dawson (16) called the shots on offense.

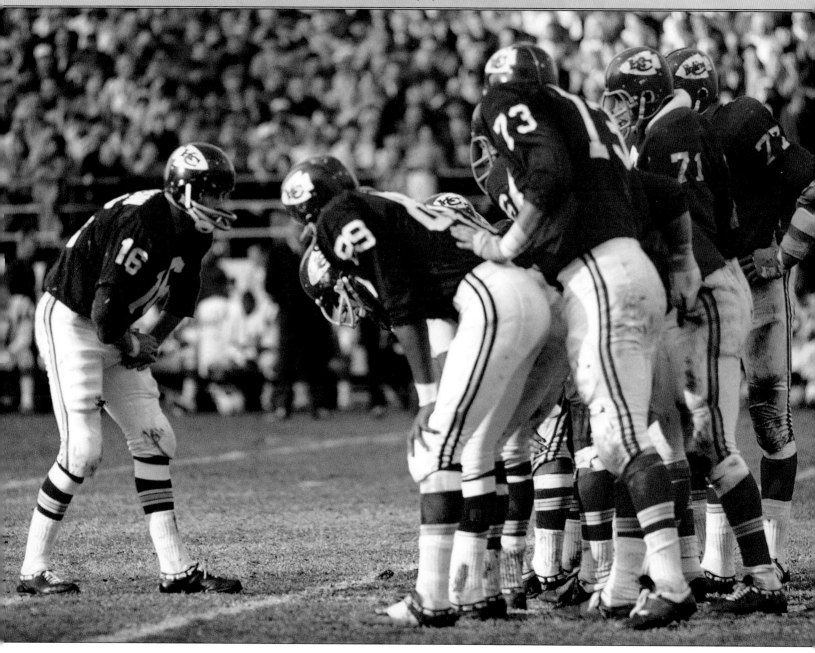

Buchanan. And the Chiefs had upgraded considerably at cornerback since their 35-10 loss to the Packers in Super Bowl I, adding Emmitt Thomas (who had an AFL-high nine interceptions) and Jim Marsalis, talented players who employed an attacking bump-and-run coverage at the corners.

Buchanan (86) and Curley Culp (opposite page) intimidated with their size. Otis Taylor (below) impressed with his big-play ability.

with Kansas City, he threw none. Three times late in the game, the Chiefs intercepted him deep in their own territory to kill Raiders' scoring threats. (In fairness to Lamonica, he played most of the fourth quarter with a broken throwing hand, the result of contact with defensive end Aaron Brown's helmet.)

There was little doubt the key to Kansas City's playoff success would be its defense. In the first round, the Chiefs went to New York to face the defending Super Bowl-champion Jets and held them to two Jim Turner field goals in a 13-6 victory. The next week, Kansas City traveled to Oakland, which had pounded Houston, 56-7, behind six Daryle Lamonica touchdown passes. The Raiders, under first-year head coach John Madden, also had handed the Chiefs two of their regular-season losses.

Lamonica had thrown 34 regular-season touchdown passes in 1969. But in Oakland's playoff meeting

Kansas City won the game and its second Super Bowl berth, 17-7.

Minnesota provided a formidable opponent. The Vikings had reached the big game with a 27-7 victory over Cleveland, pounding for 222 rushing yards behind the hard work of Dave Osborn and Bill Brown. Minnesota's 12-2 regular-season record came with an average victory margin of 17.5 points and its challenging running game helped make the Vikings two-touchdown favorites.

But Minnesota wasn't ready for Stram's inventive 3-4 defensive front, which alternately put the 6-foot-7, 270-pound Buchanan and the 6-2, 265-pound Curley Culp directly on the nose of the relatively-small (235 pounds) Vikings center Mick Tingelhoff. Minnesota hadn't seen much of that alignment and with future Hall of Fame linebackers stacking the gaps in the defensive front, Kansas City smothered the running game. The Vikings managed just 67 yards on the ground, below even the puny average the Chiefs had allowed their AFL opponents.

To make matters worse, the Vikings were not a come-from-behind team and they were down 16-0 at halftime. Minnesota's late passing attempts were futile and Joe Kapp and Gary Cuozzo were intercepted three times.

Offensively, Stram baffled the Vikings with a new look in the backfield that disguised the direction of the Chiefs' plays. He called it the Tight I-formation because tight end Fred Arbanas lined up directly behind Dawson in the backfield, with fullback Robert Holmes behind Arbanas. Minnesota's defense, accustomed to positioning the strongside linebacker

> **With future Hall-of-Fame linebackers stacking the gaps ... Kansas City smothered the running game.**

and safety across from the tight end, couldn't even decide how to line up.

That and Stram's innovative floating pass-protection pocket, in which Dawson could roll out in one direction or the other before setting himself to throw, kept the Vikings confused all afternoon.

Dawson only put the ball in the air 17 times, completing 12 passes for 142 yards and one touchdown on a quick 5-yard hitch pattern to wide receiver Otis Taylor. Taylor caught the quick-hitter and turned it into a 46-yard score. Running back Mike Garrett added a touchdown on a 5-yard run and Jan Stenerud rounded out the Chiefs' scoring with three field goals.

Despite his mediocre statistics, Dawson walked away with MVP honors—a fitting conclusion to his own difficult season and the perfect punctuation for the team's unlikely success in 1969.

18

In 1934, the NFL, always on the lookout for fan appeal, recognized a great potential for scoring with the forward pass and put the ball on a diet. Suddenly, the round, oversized pigskin was slimmed down to a prolate spheroid with a short-axis circumference of not more than 21½ inches.

In other words, the ball became something on which the passer and the receiver finally could get a grip.

Talk about good timing for Green Bay. The very next year, Don Hutson entered the league.

By 1936, Hutson's Packers had a strong-enough handle on the new, trim little football to throw and catch it all over the field on their way to the NFL championship. The Packers won the Western Division title with a 10-1-1 record, and then beat the Boston Redskins, 21-6, in the league championship game.

And the league's first great passing combination was born in the form of quarterback/tailback Arnie Herber and Hutson, the spindly end from Alabama. Herber-to-Hutson hooked up 34 times that season for eight touchdowns. Accustomed primarily to the running games and primitive passing attacks the league had been producing in its first decade and a half, the defenses that played against the new-look Packers often were at a loss for answers. For the first time, secondaries of necessity scrambled to

Clarke Hinkle, considered by some opponents the fiercest competitor in the game, led a powerful Packers running game.

1936 Green Bay Packers

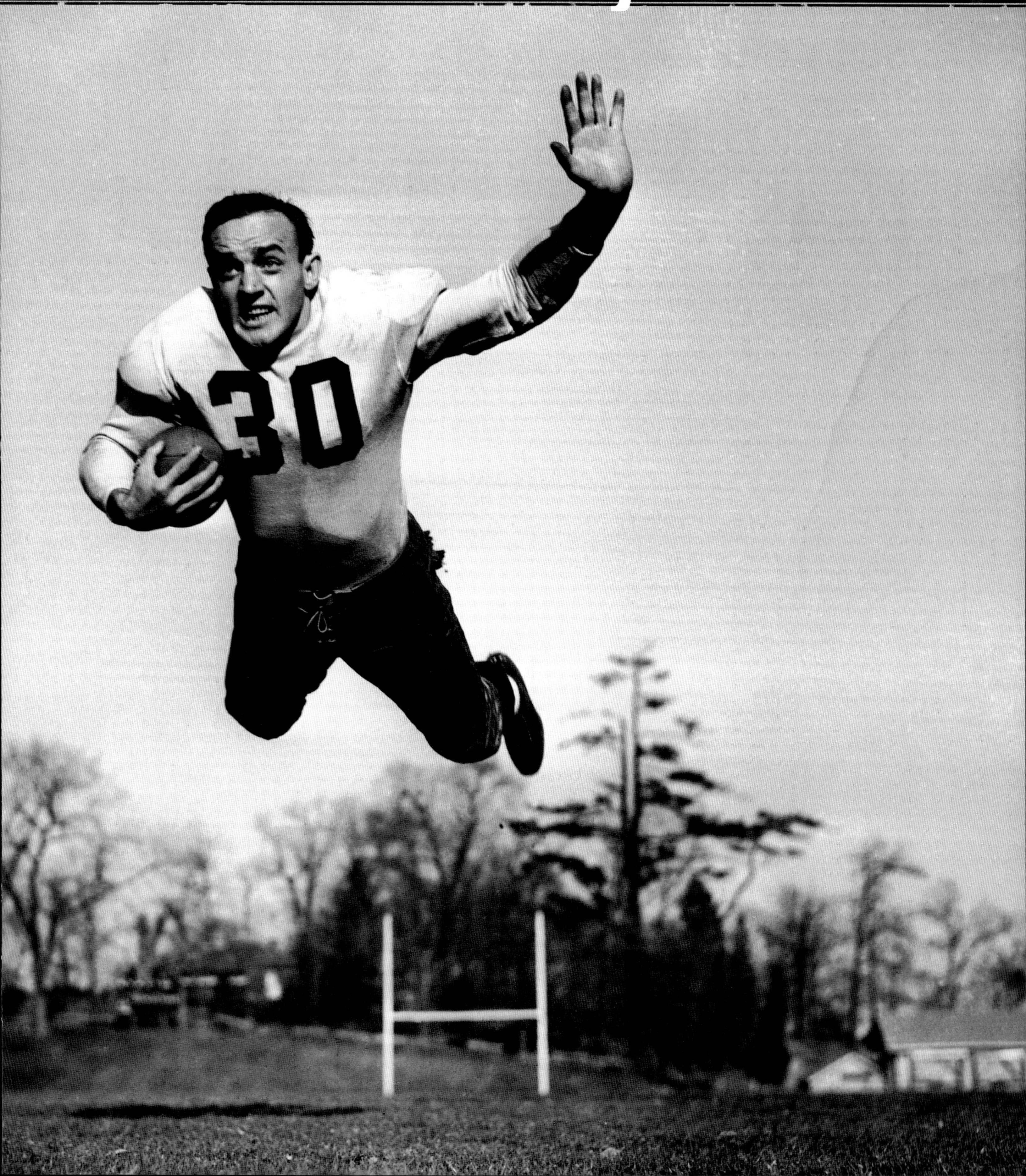

devise double- and sometimes triple-teams to cover a receiver.

Even that couldn't stop Hutson, who was fast, agile and ingenious at creating pass patterns. One veteran coach who matched up with him later in his career, the Eagles' Earle "Greasy" Neale, described Hutson as the only man who could feint in three different directions at once.

So the Packers, behind legendary coach Curly Lambeau, romped to the league title in '36 in part by taking full advantage of the new opportunities in the passing game. In addition to shrinking the size of the ball, the league had changed a key rule about forward passes in 1933—allowing the thrower to release the ball from any point behind the line of scrimmage. Until then, a passer had to be at least five yards behind the line. Lambeau, with the help of Hutson and Herber, adapted his offense to the changes more quickly than the rest of the league.

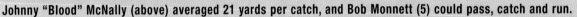

Johnny "Blood" McNally (above) averaged 21 yards per catch, and Bob Monnett (5) could pass, catch and run.

Here's how revolutionary Green Bay's passing game was in 1936:

• Herber's 1,239 passing yards broke the 3-year-old record held by the Giants' Harry Newman by 266 yards.

• Hutson's 34 receptions were eight more than any other end had ever caught in a single season. The Giants' Tod Goodwin had set the record with 26 catches in 1935.

• Hutson's 526 receiving yards shattered the previous league high by almost 100. Boston's Chuck Malone amassed 433 yards in 1935.

Hutson, of course, was just getting started in 1936. Before he finished his career in 1945, he set receiving records that would stand for the next half-century. By the early '40s, he was consistently posting receiving numbers that make his 1936 totals appear wimpy. In 1942, he caught 74 passes for 1,211 yards and 17 touchdowns and was in the middle of his remarkable streak of 95 consecutive games with at least one reception.

In 1936, though, he and the Packers were already so far ahead of the rest of the game that the Bears, Lions, Cardinals and Redskins didn't stand a chance.

This, however, was hardly a one-man team, or a one-dimensional offense. One of the great strengths of the '36 Packers was their offensive balance. Green Bay also featured Johnny "Blood" McNally (better known as Johnny Blood), who was in his final season as a player but still fleet enough to average 21 yards a catch that year. A second productive end to go with Hutson was Milt Gantenbein (15 catches for 221 yards). The threat posed by those two made the secondary's double- and triple-teams on Hutson a risky business.

When the Packers ran, they spread the ball around among three powerful backs led by fullback Clarke Hinkle, who some opponents called the fiercest competitor in the game. At

Though Don Hutson was "just getting started," he shattered league receiving records by eight catches and almost 100 yards.

To avoid double- and triple-teams on Don Hutson, coach Curly Lambeau (below) made good use of end Milt Gantenbein (above).

5-foot-11, 201 pounds, Hinkle was a pile-driver as a runner. He scored five touchdowns on the ground and rushed for 476 yards.

Bob Monnett, a small, quick back, was a triple threat. He passed (20 completions in 52 attempts for 280 yards and four TDs), rushed (224 yards) and caught the ball (13 receptions for 169 yards). George Sauer gained another 305 yards on the ground. And they all played behind guard Walt Kiesling, who at 6-2, 245, was bigger and stronger than nearly everyone he faced across the line of scrimmage.

Still, Green Bay started slowly that season. The Packers

only won their opener over the Chicago Cardinals by a field goal, 10-7. The next week, they were crushed by George Halas' Bears, who featured the great Bronko Nagurski at fullback and had many of the pieces already in place that would become the famed "Monsters of the Midway" several years later. The final score: Bears 30, Packers 3.

That, though, was their only loss. When the Packers met the Cardinals again two weeks after the opener, Green Bay won, 24-0. In a midseason rematch with the Bears, the Packers prevailed, 21-10. After that early loss, they went on a nine-game winning streak. Their only other stumble came in the last week of the regular season, when a third meeting with the Cardinals ended in a 0-0 tie.

The Bears stayed close in the standings until the last two weeks, but losses to the Lions and the Cardinals dropped them into

Arnie Herber's 1,239 passing yards broke the league's 3-year-old record by 266 yards.

second place. Green Bay went on to the championship.

The Packers ran into a bit of good luck in the title game. It had been scheduled for Boston's Fenway Park, the Redskins' home field. However, Redskins owner George Preston Marshall, in a pique over poor turnouts for Boston's previous home games, moved the championship to New York's Polo Grounds. A crowd of 29,545 showed up, but it wasn't the partisan throng that normally cheers on the home favorites and makes life miserable for the road team. (By the start of the 1937 season, Marshall's Redskins were calling Washington, D.C., home.)

Too, Boston lost one of its best players to injury on the 10th snap of the game. Halfback Cliff Battles, who rushed for 614 yards and five touchdowns and passed for another 242 yards and a TD during the regular season, gained 18 yards on his first two carries. But he didn't play after the injury.

In the first quarter, Herber and Hutson worked their magic for the Packers on a 50-yard touchdown pass. Later, Herber and Gantenbein connected on a 5-yard touchdown pass set up by a 52-yard completion to Johnny Blood, and Monnett finished the scoring with a 3-yard run in the fourth quarter.

The Packers rolled to two other championships while Hutson was in uniform, taking the crown in 1939 and again in 1944. The 1936 team, though, is significant for its introduction of the game's first modern-style passing attack.

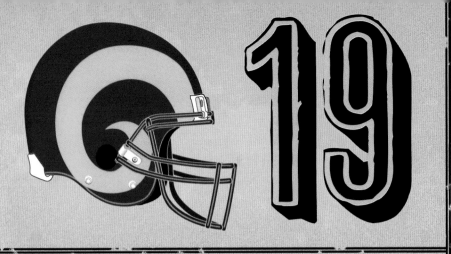

19

One question kept following the 1999 St. Louis Rams through their drive to a Super Bowl XXXIV victory, a question the rest of the National Football League asked over and over and over again all the way through the Rams' 13-3 season:

Who ARE those guys?

The question was legitimate. Never has a less likely group of players from a less likely franchise emerged from a less likely situation to win the Super Bowl. Yet the Rams did it, stopping a furious Tennessee Titans' drive six inches from the goal line as the gun sounded to secure a Super Bowl victory, 23-16.

Offensively, they came out of nowhere to torture defenses across the league. The Super Bowl may have been won by only half a foot when St. Louis linebacker Mike Jones tackled Tennessee wide receiver Kevin Dyson inside the 1-yard line, but nearly every other victory during the Rams' incredible season came by miles and miles. St. Louis scored 526 points, an average of almost 33 per game, and gave up less than half that. The average margin of victory was a laughably-comfortable 17.8 points.

In many ways, the Rams' story defied belief. Throughout the '90s, they were one of the most hapless franchises in the league, first as representatives of Los Angeles and then, beginning in 1995, of St. Louis. Until 1999, no team had won fewer games in the decade and they had finished last in the NFC Western Division in seven of the nine seasons. Their two

The Rams were an offensive machine, but it was a defensive stop—by Mike Jones (52)—that won the Super Bowl by inches.

third-place finishes (1995 and '96) were accomplished with 7-9 and 6-10 records.

They were coming off a 4-12 record and last place finish in 1998. To make matters worse, Trent Green, the free-agent quarterback brought in after the '98 season to turn the team around, tore up a knee during an exhibition game in August and was lost for the year.

When Green went down, offensive coordinator Mike Martz, himself a no-namer who had been laboring in obscurity tutoring quarterbacks for the Redskins until Rams' head coach Dick Vermeil brought him to St. Louis before the '99 season, was in the process of installing a new passing attack. It was a lightning-quick, daring, highly-complex and wide-open offense that depended on speed and timing and the

instincts of the quarterback for success.

And now, at the last moment, Martz and Vermeil had to turn to Kurt Warner to run it.

Warner, who had learned his pro football lessons in the backwaters of the Arena Football League while playing for the Iowa Barnstormers.

Warner, whose most recent football experience had come in the NFL's version of baseball's bush leagues—NFL Europe, where he was a member of the Amsterdam Admirals.

Warner, who once tried out for the Green Bay Packers and was told, in essence, "come back when you grow up, kid."

Warner, who figured so lightly in the Rams' plans that he had been made available to the expansion Cleveland Browns on St. Louis' draft-eligible list. Even the Browns didn't want him.

That Kurt Warner. No wonder the Rams took the NFL by surprise.

Warner didn't waste any time. In St. Louis' opener against the Colts, he put the ball in the air 44 times, completed 28 passes, gained 316 yards and threw for three touchdowns. The Rams beat one of the best defenses in the league, 27-10.

In the second game, against Atlanta, he passed for another three touchdowns and 275 yards. The next week, Warner scorched the Bengals for 310 yards and three more passing touchdowns. And he was just warming up.

On October 10 at home against the 49ers, in the Rams' fourth game, Warner hooked up with wide receiver Isaac Bruce on three touchdown passes in the first quarter alone. By the time he finished that afternoon's work, he had thrown five scoring passes, including a fourth to Bruce, on 20 completions in 23 attempts for 323 yards. And St. Louis won, 42-20.

The Rams were on their way to six straight victories to open the season. The rest of the league was starting to get curious. What's going on in St. Louis? Who are those guys?

"Those guys" were running the most sophisticated offense in the league, a 21st-century version of Don Coryell's vertical passing attack from the '70s and '80s, enhanced by the best all-purpose running back in football. Marshall Faulk, who joined the Rams in a trade with Indianapolis during the offseason, broke the NFL's record for total yards from scrimmage that year. He gained 1,381 yards on the ground and another 1,048 yards from a team-leading 87 receptions.

Faulk was spectacular in the open field, and the Rams' offense was built to get him the ball where the field was open.

Faulk's running and catching, along with four of the fastest wide receivers in football, gave Warner weapons at every skill position. Bruce caught 77 passes for 1,165 yards and 12 touchdowns. Rookie wide receiver Torry Holt caught 52 for 788 yards and six scores. Az-Zahir Hakim brought another pair of fleet feet to the receiving corps, and counted eight touchdowns among his 36 receptions for 677 yards. Ricky Proehl, the fourth wide receiver, added 33 catches for 349 yards.

The Rams' high-tech offense starred Kurt Warner (opposite page), wide receiver Isaac Bruce (80) and running back Marshall Faulk (below).

The playbook was a weighty tome chock-full of deep crossing patterns, throwback passes, screens, draw plays, delay routes, shifts, motion and every other form of mischief that might bedevil a defense. Warner had as many as six options on every pass play, which ought to have made the system extremely challenging for an unproven quarterback. Instead, he shocked the league with his immediate mastery of it.

By the end of the season, he had thrown for 4,353 yards and 41 touchdowns, leading the NFL in both categories. Only Miami's Dan Marino had ever thrown for more TDs in a single season.

The Rams lost twice at midseason by a total of seven points. They dropped a 24-21 decision to Tennessee on Halloween despite 328 passing yards from Warner and 415 yards of total offense. Jeff Wilkins missed a field goal in the closing moments that would have tied it. The next week, a last-minute touchdown pass from Detroit's Gus Frerotte to Johnnie Morton sent St. Louis to its second consecutive defeat, 31-27.

The only other loss was a meaningless season finale at Philadelphia, in which the

Grant Wistrom (98) and Orlando Pace (76) were key figures on opposite sides of the line.

Rams, playing mostly backups after the first half, turned the ball over seven times.

Warner and the offense were at their very best in the first round of the playoffs against the Vikings. Warner connected on 27 of his 33 passes for 391 yards, and threw almost as many touchdown passes (five) as incompletions. St. Louis scored 35 points in the second half and romped, 49-37.

The NFC Championship Game posed a tougher challenge, as Tampa Bay came to St. Louis with the league's No. 3 defense. The Bucs played a seamless zone that kept Warner from finding the one-on-one matchups in the secondary that had been so common against Minnesota. Still, he passed for 258 yards and found Proehl open late in the game for the Rams' only touchdown. Meanwhile, Tampa Bay's conservative offense did next to nothing against a St. Louis defense that ranked first in the league against the run. The Rams won, 11-6.

Then came the Super Bowl. Warner was magnificent again, setting a Super Bowl record with 414 passing yards and two touchdowns. His second scoring pass covered 73 yards deep down the right sideline to Bruce with just over two minutes to play, and broke a 16-16 tie.

By that time, the rest of the league knew the answer to the question it had been asking all season.

Those guys? Those guys are the World Champions.

Defensive linemen D'Marco Farr (75) and Kevin Carter (93) celebrate a division title with Faulk.

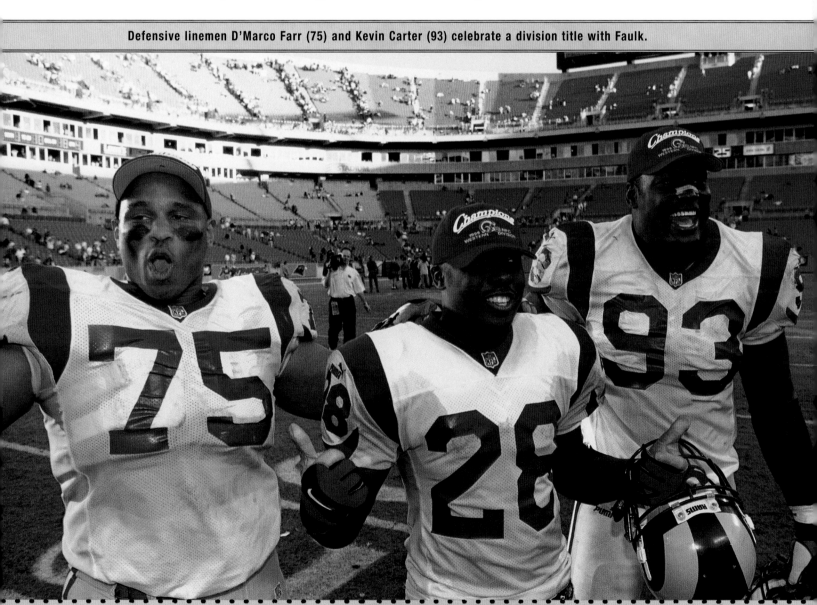

20

The drama in the young National Football League's 1929 season is best described in a tale of two cities.

In one little corner of the professional football world was Green Bay, Wis. For the first time, the tiny-town Packers were preparing to flex the muscle that has made them one of the league's most successful and storied franchises. Before 1929, they had fielded good teams, but never one capable of winning a championship.

And in another very large corner of the pro football world was New York City, where Gotham's Giants were already building a tradition of excellence. The Giants won the league title in 1927 with an 11-1-1 record and were primed to challenge for another.

Those two teams, and those two cities, were destined to battle for the 1929 championship; and on November 24 in front of an estimated crowd of 25,000 at New York's Polo Grounds, they put on quite a show.

The Packers prevailed that day by a 20-6 score, and then finished out their final three games without a loss. Because the league didn't play an official title game until 1933, Green Bay became the 1929 champion, the first of its 12 NFL titles, on the strength of its 12-0-1 record. The Giants finished second at 13-1-1.

Getting those two teams to that November 24 showdown is a story in itself, one that makes today's era of free agency and player movement look like a model of stability.

In 1928, the Packers had finished 6-4-3 and in the middle of the league standings. So as he prepared for

Player/coach Curly Lambeau built one of the NFL's first dynasties, winning the league title in 1929, 1930 and 1931.

1929 Green Bay Packers

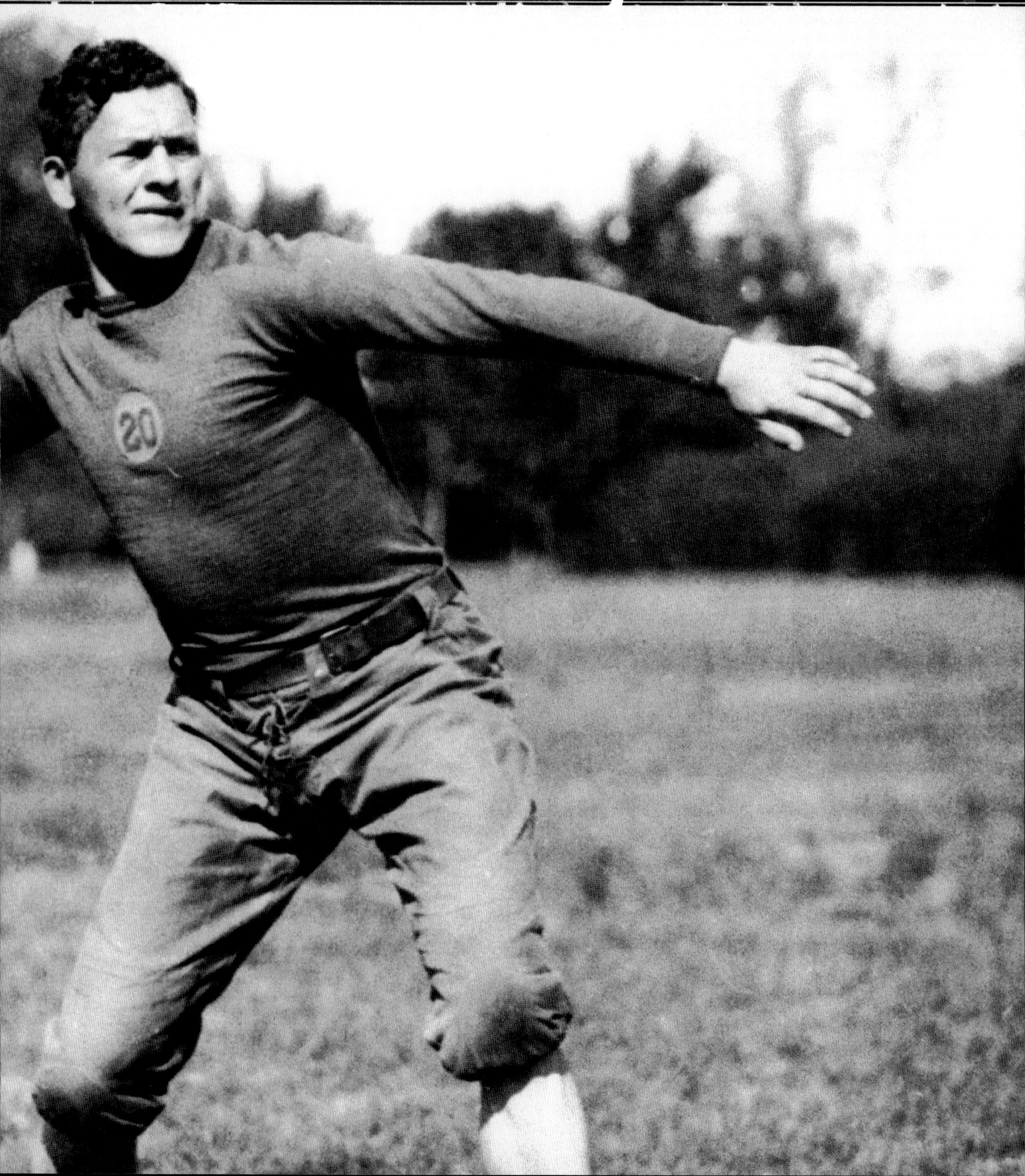

Cal Hubbard (22), shown in this 1933 photo, provided a huge lift to the Packers' defense.

the following season, player/coach Curly Lambeau knew he needed help. He acquired three new players in 1929, and all three eventually became Hall of Famers: massive lineman Cal Hubbard, lineman/linebacker "Iron" Mike Michalske and free-spirited back Johnny "Blood" McNally.

That trio formed the nucleus of one of the NFL's first dynasties. The Packers not only won the 1929 title, but also took the league championships in 1930 and '31.

Hubbard, who was variously listed anywhere from 6-foot-2 to 6-foot-5 and weighed in the 250-pound range, was the key. His acquisition is especially notable because Lambeau took him away from the Giants with a lobbying effort that today would have the league's tampering rules invoked before the morning coffee turned cold.

Early in the 1928 season, Lambeau watched Hubbard play for the Giants in New York's 6-0 victory over Green Bay. From that day forward, Lambeau talked long and loud about his desire to have Hubbard, the game's first super-sized hero, play for the Packers.

Hubbard, who wasn't happy with the New York lifestyle, listened. Eventually, he went to Giants owner Tim Mara with a let-me-go-or-I-quit ultimatum. He soon became a Packer. (In 1936, Hubbard returned to the Giants. After his playing days, he became a baseball umpire and eventually was inducted in baseball's Hall of Fame, making him the only person to be enshrined at both Cooperstown and Canton.)

Lambeau picked up Michalske as a true free agent when the New York Yankees folded after the 1928 season. For the Packers, Michalske became the best two-way guard in the NFL, and developed a particularly imposing reputation on defense for his ferocity in rushing the passer. That ability was especially important against the Giants on November 24.

McNally, more often known by his adopted nickname of Johnny Blood, came to Green Bay when another team, the Pottsville Maroons, went out of business. Lambeau lured him with the promise of $100 a week, and then upped the offer to $110 if

Verne Lewellen was an important piece in Green Bay's 1929 backfield puzzle.

Red Dunn (above) provided depth to the backfield, but Johnny Blood (below) was the Packers biggest threat.

the hard-drinking, hard-living halfback would promise to give up the booze after Tuesday of every week. Blood allegedly said, "I'll take the $100." In any event, he became a Packer. For the next 10 seasons, he was one of the fastest backs and best receivers in the league, even as he drank, caroused and womanized his way through his playing days.

With those three leading the way, Green Bay dominated its opponents in 1929, particularly defensively. The Packers recorded eight shutouts and allowed only 22 points all season. They were more than just good. They were intimidating, especially when Hubbard glared across the line of scrimmage at an offense.

Hubbard, so the legend

goes, once gave this bit of friendly advice to a new teammate about the "proper" use of the ear-holes in the other team's helmets: "They're not to hear through. They're for you to stick your fingers in his helmet and jerk his face down when you raise your knee up."

For all of Lambeau's personnel shuffling before the 1929 season began, Mara may have outdone him. Lambeau brought in three new players. Mara bought an entire team to meld with his existing troops.

Mostly, the Giants' owner wanted one player —tailback Benny Friedman, who had been revolutionizing the game with his penchant for passing out of the single-wing formation, first at

Mike Michalske (above) and Lavie Dilweg (below) were big contributors to the Packers cause.

the University of Michigan and then for the short-lived Cleveland Bulldogs and Detroit Wolverines of the NFL. Detroit would not trade Friedman to the Giants, so Mara bought the whole franchise for $10,000. Friedman became a Giant, along with six of his Detroit teammates and the Wolverines' coach, LeRoy Andrews.

Friedman's passing efficiency was unparalleled at the time. Unlike the game's other throwers, he put the ball in the air on any down and from any spot on the field. By the time the 1929 season ended, Friedman had thrown an unprecedented 20 touchdown passes for New York. The Giants rolled undefeated (8-0-1) through their first nine games, as their opponents wrestled unsuccessfully with how to stop the newfangled offensive attack.

Then they met the 9-0 Packers at the Polo Grounds. Friedman managed one touchdown pass, a 6-yard completion to Tony Plansky. But Green Bay, behind a ferocious rush from Hubbard and Michalske, harried him into his worst outing of the year.

Twice, Friedman threw critical interceptions, including one into Hubbard's arms at the Packers' 1-yard line just after a 65-yard completion to end Ray Flaherty. The second interception came late in the fourth quarter and led to Green

Bay's last touchdown.

The Packers may not have had the sleek passing offense that Freidman's Giants brought to the game, but they were balanced and powerful when they had the ball. They didn't score more than 25 points in any of their 13 games, but they spread the ball around among Blood and the other backs, including Verne Lewellen, Bo Molenda and Red Dunn, as well as end Lavie Dilweg.

The defense did the rest. Green Bay only allowed three touchdowns all season. In fact, Friedman's TD pass to Plansky on Nov. 24 tallied the last points the Packers gave up in 1929.

The one minor blemish on Green Bay's 1929 record occurred just four days after the Giants game in the Polo Grounds. Trying to make the most of the long train trip to the East Coast, Lambeau scheduled three games in eight days before the team headed home. On November 28, the Thursday after the Sunday game in New York, the Packers played to a 0-0 tie with the Frankford Yellowjackets, a team from a Philadelphia suburb.

The next Sunday, December 1, Green Bay took the field again, this time in Providence against the Steam Roller. The Packers won, 25-0, and all was right with the world once more. Or, at least, with Green Bay's little corner of it.

21

They had answers. The 1991 Washington Redskins nearly always had the answers. They had the personnel to answer physical challenges from across the line of scrimmage, and they had the coaching staff to answer tactical maneuvers from the braintrust across the field.

The Redskins won their first 11 games and Super Bowl XXVI because they had a response for every gimmicky offense and every tricky defense the rest of the league threw at them. And they saw a lot of gimmicks, a lot of tricks. Whether it was the nine-man defensive front that Atlanta tried in the middle of the year or the no-huddle offense that carried Buffalo into the Super Bowl, the Redskins had an answer at the ready.

They were a running team first. That was the way coach Joe Gibbs wanted to play it, and that was what opposing defenses prepared to stop. So when the Falcons questioned Washington's ability to throw the ball in a November game by stacking the line of scrimmage with every available body to stop the run, the Redskins answered with a 442-yard, six-touchdown passing day from quarterback Mark Rypien. Four of those TDs came from 60-or-more yards out, as Atlanta tried to contain wide receivers Gary Clark and Art Monk with man-to-man coverage. Washington won, 56-17.

When the power running game of Earnest Byner

Running back Earnest Byner (right) led a well-balanced Redskins offense with 1,048 rushing yards and five touchdowns.

1991 Washington Redskins

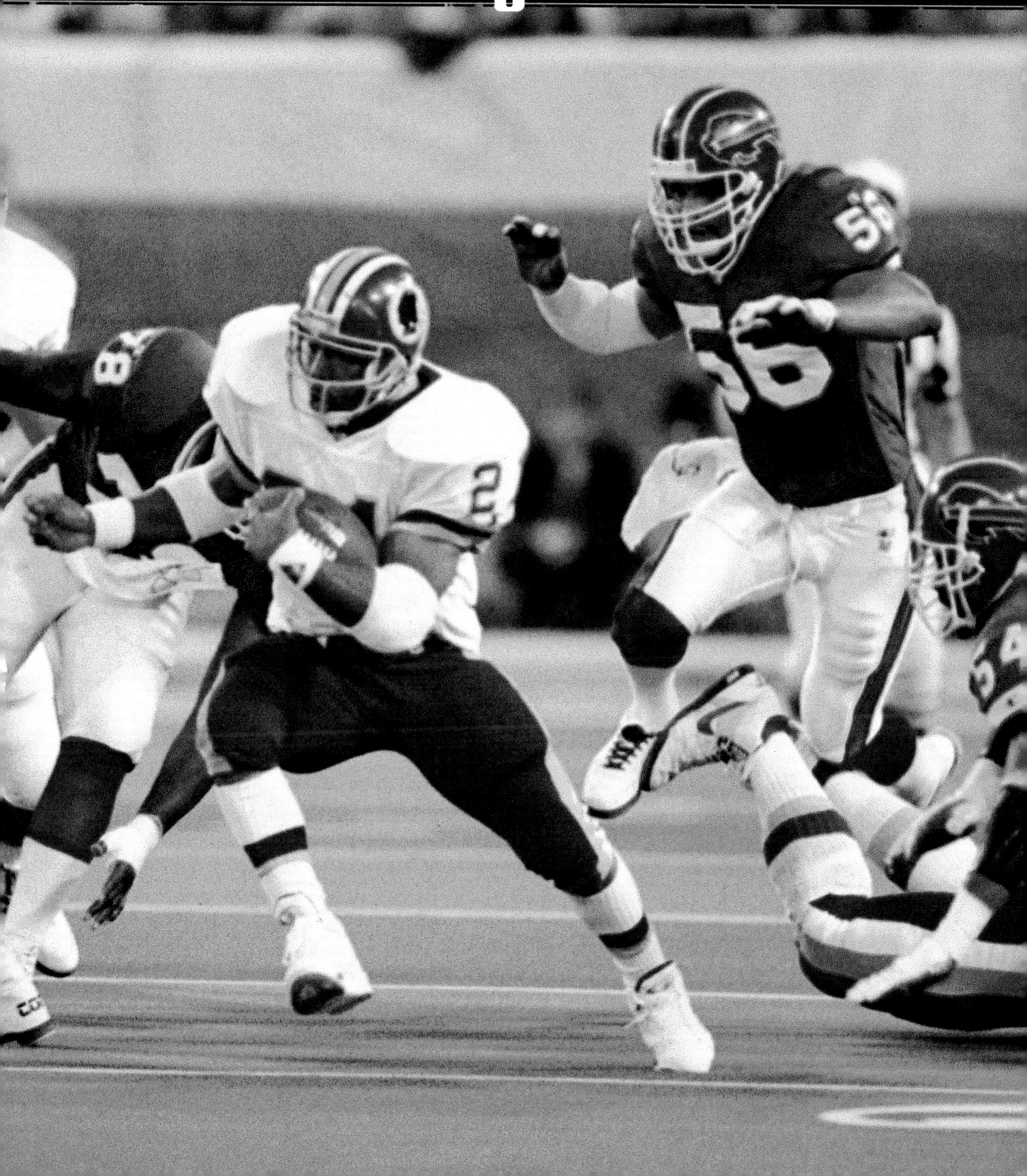

wasn't there between the tackles—and it wasn't in the second half of an October game against the Browns—the Redskins answered with the outside speed of rookie running back Ricky Ervins. In 13 second-half carries

When the running game sputtered, quarterback Mark Rypien went to work.

against Cleveland that day, Ervins gained 133 yards and scored two touchdowns as Washington cake-walked to a 42-17 victory.

In the biggest game of the year, Gibbs knew his defense would be matching Super Bowl wits with Marv Levy's no-huddle offense.

Buffalo's attack allowed quarterback Jim Kelly to call formations and plays at the line of scrimmage rather than in the huddle, and it helped the Bills lead the league in total yardage in 1991. Kelly led the league in touchdown passes with 33, Thurman Thomas led the AFC in rushing and Buffalo scored more points than every team except Washington.

One of the reasons the Bills' no-huddle worked so well is that it minimized the defense's situational substitutions. It didn't allow enough time between plays for the defense to change its personnel when down and distance called for either an obvious pass or an obvious run. Because the Redskins did more situational substituting than most teams, some questioned their ability to adjust.

As usual, Gibbs had an answer. The Redskins had dabbled with their own no-huddle attack off and on during the season, although Gibbs hadn't used it for much more than the occasional hurry-up drive at the close of a half. During Washington's preparation for the Super Bowl, he made it more of a priority for his starting offense. That way, he learned that the Bills would be able to run plays as often as every 20-to-22 seconds, which in turn taught defensive coordinator Richie Petitbon how quickly he would need to shuffle his players onto the field. As a result, the Redskins were still able to use a variety of different fronts and looks against Buffalo.

They intercepted Kelly four times, sacked him five times and batted away five of his passes at the line of scrimmage. The

Redskins outgained Buffalo 417 to 283 in total yardage, and outscored the Bills 37-24.

Plus, Washington's new no-huddle offense, which Gibbs used on several series, proved to be an effective weapon against an unsuspecting Bills' defense.

That was an emphatic answer.

As the Redskins rolled to a 14-2 regular-season record, they averaged more than 30 points per game behind a balanced running attack and Rypien's career-best 3,564 passing yards and 28 touchdowns. Byner rushed for 1,048 yards and five touchdowns; Ervins for 680 yards and three TDs. In short yardage and near the goal line, they turned to Gerald Riggs. He gained only 248 yards, but scored 11 touchdowns.

Monk and Clark both surpassed 1,000 yards in receptions and combined for 18 TDs. Ricky Sanders, Washington's third wide receiver, kept the cornerbacks honest and, most of the time, out of man-to-man coverage with his 45 receptions for 580 yards and another five touchdowns.

The real stars of the offensive show, though, were "The Hogs," Washington's celebrated offensive line. Tackles Jim Lachey and Joe Jacoby, guards Raleigh McKenzie and Mark Schlereth and center Jeff Bostic were all veterans and all leaders. They were the perfect fit in a Gibbs system that called on linemen to block not only for a power running attack, but also for Rypien's extensive play-action passing game.

Rypien threw 421 passes. He was sacked only seven times. Backup quarterback Jeff Rutledge was sacked twice. Nine sacks, all season long. No wonder The Hogs were as venerated in Washington as Byner, Rypien, Clark and Monk.

Together, the offense and defense, which ranked second in the league, gave the Redskins an average victory margin of 16.3 points. No team had won more games by a

Rypien's favorite targets were Gary Clark (above) and Art Monk (below).

Linebacker Andre Collins (below) was a key figure in Washington's swarming defense.

wider margin in more than 20 years. Their two losses—to Dallas in the season's 12th game and to Philadelphia in a meaningless season finale—were by a total of five points.

The playoffs were a tour de force for the defense. Despite a divisional-round downpour, the Falcons chose to attack with a wide-open passing game. Washington's defense intercepted four Atlanta passes. The Redskins wisely kept mostly to the ground, and Riggs scored twice from in close in a 24-7 victory.

In the 41-10 win over Detroit for the NFC championship, Washington's defense forced two turnovers on the Lions' first seven offensive plays to launch the Redskins to a 10-0 lead. Cornerback Darrell Green returned a fourth-quarter interception for another touchdown.

Then came the four interceptions and five sacks against Kelly and the Bills in the Super Bowl.

As with most good teams, luck played a role for the Redskins every now and then. They were lucky when Houston's Ian Howfield missed a 33-yard field-goal attempt with four seconds to go in the ninth game of the season and left the score tied 13-13. Chip Lohmiller didn't miss his field-goal try in overtime, and Washington won, 16-13.

They were lucky, too, when the Cowboys' Emmitt Smith took ill during the season's second game. He gained 112 yards on his first 11 carries, but didn't play the rest of the way. Washington held on, 33-31. And perhaps luck had something to do with the Lions' Barry Sanders missing the season opener, although even Sanders couldn't have undone the 45-0 rout in RFK Stadium. Four-and-a-half months later, Sanders was on the field at RFK for the rematch in the NFC Championship Game, and the outcome didn't change.

The Redskins were even a little lucky at the start of the Super Bowl when Buffalo's Thomas, the NFL's offensive player of the year, spent the Bills' first two plays on the sideline rather than the field, scurrying up and down the bench in search of his missing helmet. Thomas led the league in total yards from scrimmage that year—1,407 rushing yards and another 631 on 62 receptions—but the "Case of the Missing Headgear" seemed to affect his Super Bowl productivity. He was hardly more effective with his helmet than

he had been on the sideline without it: 10 carries for 13 yards, four catches for another 27.

Luck, though, had nothing to do with Washington's answer to the blitzing pressure the Bills tried to put on Rypien and the passing game. Buffalo's pass rush came at the expense of coverage on Monk and Clark, so as long as "The Hogs" contained the pressure, Rypien would find open receivers.

They did, and he did. Rypien's 292 passing yards and two touchdowns made him the Super Bowl MVP. Clark caught seven passes for 114 yards and a TD; Monk had seven catches for 113 yards.

And Rypien wasn't sacked. The "Answer Men" had done it again.

Safety Brad Edwards (27) and the Redskins defense brought Buffalo's productive offense back to earth in the Super Bowl.

22

The NFL might not have seen the 1986 Giants coming, at least not early in the season. New York racked up wins, to be sure. But the wins weren't the kind of pulverizing knockouts that would cause, say, the defending Super Bowl-champion Bears or the proud 49ers to cover up and cry "No mas! No mas!"

Instead, the Giants won those early games by five measly points against the Raiders, by three against the Saints, by a touchdown over the Cardinals and the Redskins, by a field goal over the Cowboys and Eagles. They beat the Vikings 22-20 and needed a late fourth-and-17 completion from Phil Simms to Bobby Johnson to do it.

In many cases, these were opponents ripe for a hay-maker the Giants didn't deliver. The Raiders, Saints, Cardinals, Cowboys, Eagles—none of them finished the season with a winning record. And yet, the Giants were just surviving against them, not crushing them.

They lost to Dallas, 31-28, in the season opener, a Monday Night Football game at Texas Stadium, and the Cowboys stumbled on to a 7-9 record. The Giants lost to a good Seattle team, 17-12, in the seventh week of the season.

Even into December, the Giants weren't playing like a powerhouse. On December 1, San Francisco took a 17-0 lead into halftime against them at Candlestick Park. But the Saints rallied to win, 21-17, with a late

Mark Bavaro (89) bulls forward after making one of his four Super Bowl catches against Denver.

1986 New York Giants

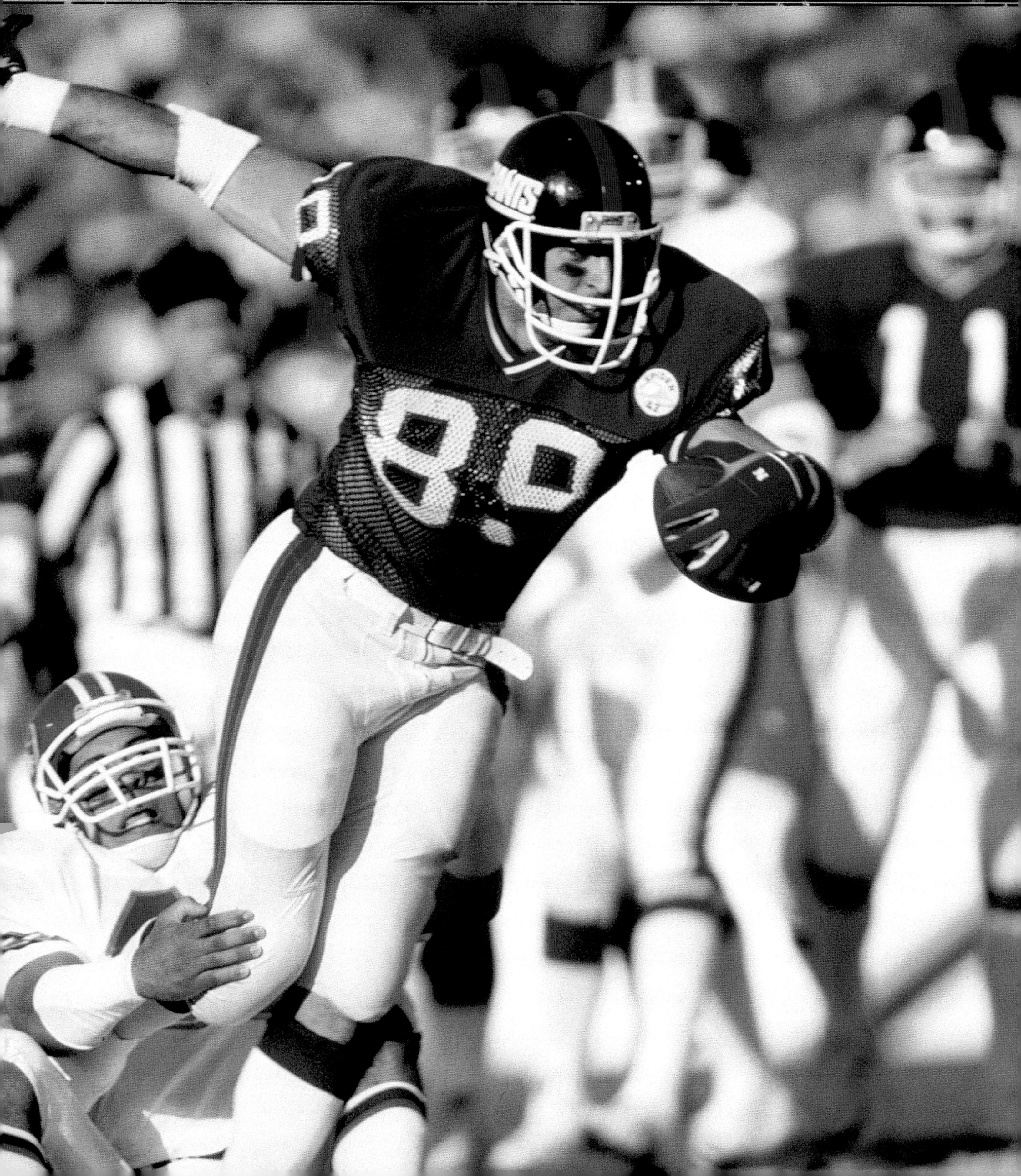

49-yard Simms-to-Stacy Robinson bomb that set up Ottis Anderson's 1-yard touchdown run. Another escape.

Certainly, the AFC champion Broncos didn't see New York coming, not after the Giants had sneaked another notch into the win column. The Giants' 19-16 victory on November 23 left Denver players unimpressed—a mindset that would come into play when the same two teams squared off in Super Bowl XXI.

That November look, though, bore absolutely no resemblance to the dominance the Giants showed their last five opponents. Starting with a 27-7 victory over St. Louis on December 14, New York thundered over

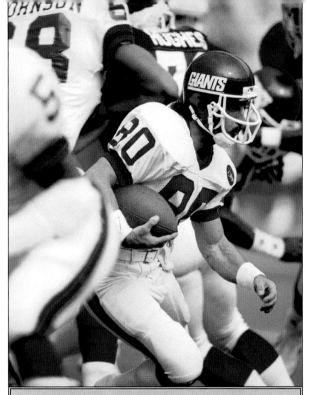

Phil Simms (below) had plenty of targets, including diminutive wideout Phil McConkey (80).

everything in its path.

The season ended with a 55-24 victory over Green Bay and the playoffs began with a 49-3 obliteration of San Francisco, the team that had taken a 17-0 halftime lead just five weeks earlier.

The postseason continued with a 17-0 thumping of the Redskins in the NFC Championship Game.

And the Super Bowl . . . well, the Broncos may still be wondering what hit them. Denver actually led 10-9 at halftime, but New York scored 17 points in the third quarter while the Broncos gained a total of two yards. Another 13 points in the fourth quarter completed a 39-20 blowout and gave the Giants

George Martin (75) charged QBs and Joe Morris (below) charged defenses, rushing for 1,516 yards.

their first NFL title in 30 years.

In its last five games, New York outscored opponents 187-54. It was as if head coach Bill Parcells had his team playing possum until the games and the season reached their most meaningful points.

After a fashion, that's what Parcells did with his offense. For a good part of the year, he fostered the perception that the Giants were a traditional power running team, with a passing game that was ancillary. It was an easy subterfuge, because New York ran the ball with as much authority as smashmouth teams of NFL yore. One of the Giants' favorite plays, in fact, looked an awful lot like the famous "Packer Sweep" of Vince Lombardi's Green Bay days. Guards Billy Ard and Chris Godfrey pulled, and fullback Maurice Carthon led halfback

Joe Morris around the end.

Morris rushed for 1,516 yards and scored 14 touchdowns on the ground behind a big and experienced offensive line that featured Ard and Godfrey at guards, Bart Oates at center and Karl Nelson and Brad Benson at tackles. It was a punishing, and efficent, brand of football, even if it didn't lead to many three-touchdown victories in the season's first few months.

At quarterback, Simms quietly put together some impressive passing numbers during the regular season. He threw for 3,487 yards and 21 touchdowns, completing 55.3 percent of his attempts. Those statistics even matched up nicely with his higher-profile Super Bowl counterpart, the Broncos' John Elway, who completed 55.6 percent of his passes for 19 touchdowns and

3,485 yards.

Nonetheless, the Giants came into the Super Bowl with a reputation as a muscle-up running club. Even though Simms had thrown five touchdown passes in New York's two playoff games, including four in the 49-3 first-round romp over San Francisco, the Giants weren't putting the ball in the air any more frequently than they had earlier in the season.

Many people—including, apparently, the Broncos—failed to notice how efficiently Simms was using the relatively few passes he threw down the season's stretch. Denver opened the Super Bowl in man-to-man coverage, preferring to focus on Morris and Carthon.

There had hardly been a need to turn Simms loose, the way New York's defense played. The Giants boasted the top rushing defense in the league, allowing only 80 yards per game, and most teams knew better than to attack them in that manner. But passing was risky business, too, because Lawrence Taylor, Gary Reasons, team captain Harry Carson and leading tackler Carl Banks formed the most imposing linebacker unit in the league. Outside man Taylor led the NFL

Lawrence Taylor (above) led a defense that also featured Harry Carson, Martin (75) and Carl Banks (58).

Ottis Anderson's fourth-quarter touchdown plunge dashed Denver's hopes of a Super Bowl comeback.

with $20\frac{1}{2}$ sacks.

Only the Bears, who were still mashing offenses with the "46" defense that had taken them to the Super Bowl championship a year earlier, allowed fewer points in 1986 than the Giants' 236, an average of just under 15 per game.

New York's defense experienced perhaps it finest moment in the first half of the Super Bowl, when the Broncos moved to a first down at the 1-yard line and failed to score. Taylor threw Elway for a loss on first down. The middle of the Giants' defense smothered running back Gerald Willhite on second down. Banks nailed Sammy Winder trying to run to his left on third down. And Rich Karlis missed a short field goal on fourth down.

The strength of the defense fed the perception that the Giants played a power game on offense. It was a tried-and-true formula: defense and the run win Super Bowls.

So Denver didn't expect what Simms showed them. He came out throwing. More to the point, he came out throwing successfully. Nine times in the first half, he even threw on first down. By comparison, Parcells called first-down running plays only three times through the first two quarters.

At halftime, Morris had only carried the ball seven times for 36 yards.

When he was finished, Simms had missed on only three of his 25 passes. His 88 percent completion rate was a Super Bowl record, as he shredded Denver's man-to-man coverage, especially in the first half, for 268 yards. Incredibly, he threw as many touchdown passes as incompletions. Tight end Mark Bavaro caught a 13-yard TD pass, and Zeke Mowatt and Phil McConkey each caught 6-yard touchdown tosses.

When the game ended, Simms was on a streak of 10 straight completions. He played, Parcells said, perhaps the best game any quarterback has ever played.

Who could have seen that coming?

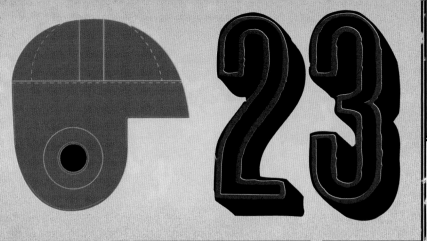

23

Wilbur Henry weighed 250 pounds, by some estimates, and went by the nickname of "Fats." Henry played tackle for the Canton Bulldogs back in 1923, the NFL's second season and he played it well enough to be in the inaugural class of 17 enshrinees when the Pro Football Hall of Fame opened in 1963. That means he brought a level of line talent to the Bulldogs that the other 19 teams in the infant league couldn't match.

Henry, who also went by the nickname "Pete," brought another element to the game, too. On occasion, he brought his 6-foot frame, powerful legs, quick feet and 250 pounds to Canton's backfield. He was William "Refrigerator" Perry some six decades before Perry took the pro football world by storm when he lined up occasionally in the Chicago Bears backfield.

When Canton needed a power ballcarrier, player/coach Guy Chamberlin sometimes turned to his standout two-way tackle. The Bulldogs occasionally even used Fats as a tackle-eligible receiver back in 1923. The NFL was only 2 years old (4, if you count the 1920 and '21 seasons, when a number of independent teams, including Canton, came together as the American Professional Football Association),

The Bulldogs, who finished 10-0-2 in 1922 and 11-0-1 in 1923, were the NFL's first powerhouse team.

but the men who masterminded it had already dreamed up a trick play or two.

And the list of Henry's accomplishments for the 1923 Bulldogs goes on. He scored a touchdown on a reception, drop-kicked nine field goals and led the league with 25 extra-point drop-kicks.

Henry and his fellow tackle, Roy "Link" Lyman, were the undisputed stars on the NFL's first powerhouse team. In both 1922

Wilbur "Fats" Henry sometimes slipped into the backfield when the Bulldogs needed a power rusher.

and 1923, the Bulldogs dominated a league of mostly-Midwestern teams, cruising unbeaten through those two seasons. Canton was 10-0-2 in 1922, 11-0-1 in 1923.

Back when the NFL was that young, nobody thought much about statistics. So the history left by the Bulldogs doesn't offer much in the way of individual achievements. We don't know about rushing yards, passing yards, receiving yards.

But we know scores. And we don't have to look very far down the column of results from the 1923 season to know how Canton earned its place in the annals of the league's very best teams.

In 12 games, the Bulldogs scored 246 points. That's an average of 20.5 per game, which would hold up as a pretty fair offensive output even by today's standards.

But Canton's most impressive legacy is its defense. The Bulldogs allowed a total of 19 points in the entire 1923 season, an average of 1.6 points per game. No one scored on them until the fifth

game of the year, and that was a field goal by the Akron Indians in a 7-3 Canton victory.

Only once that season did a team cross the goal line against the Bulldogs. The Cleveland Indians managed a touchdown and a field goal on November 25 at Dunn Field in Cleveland in front of an estimated 17,000 fans. That crowd, thought to be the largest in the NFL's young history to that point, watched Canton roll to a 46-10 victory.

(Three NFL teams in 1923 were nicknamed the Indians. The third was Jim Thorpe's club made up entirely of Native Americans, named the Oorang Indians. Thorpe had played for the Bulldogs from 1915-20.)

Before we lionize Canton's defense, however, we should point out that shutouts weren't unusual during those early years of the NFL. Because the ball was bigger than it is today and consequently more difficult to pass, scoring happened much less frequently. Among the 99 NFL games during the 1923 season, 56

> ## No one scored on them until the fifth game of the year, and that was a field goal.

Roy "Link" Lyman was the first defensive lineman to shift positions just before the ball was snapped.

were shutouts. And of those 56, seven were double shutouts—games that ended 0-0.

Still, Canton's defense clearly ruled. The Bulldogs held eight of their 12 opponents scoreless.

Henry, who like most players of his day played both offense and defense, was one big reason for that strength. The other was his teammate at tackle.

Another Hall of Famer, Lyman was an innovator on the line even as the game itself was evolving out of the primordial ooze of Walter Camp's genius. Lyman developed a technique on defense that consistently confused the offense's blocking schemes and is still in use today. He was the first defensive lineman to shift positions just before the ball was snapped, gambling on his instinct for where the play was headed.

On offense, Lyman made occasional use of Chamberlin's tackle-eligible pass plays, too. He caught one

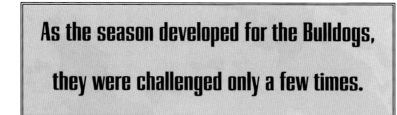

As the season developed for the Bulldogs, they were challenged only a few times.

touchdown pass in 1923.

Both Lyman and Henry were big men by the standards of the day. Although we can't count on the accuracy of the records of their weight (they were listed variously between 235 and 255 pounds), they no doubt were bigger than most of the linemen they faced. Even on the champion Bulldogs, they dwarfed the rest of the line. Guards Rudy Comstock and Duke Osborn and center Larry Conover weighed around 200 pounds. So in addition to their talent and versatility, Henry and Lyman had the advantage of size in many of Canton's matchups.

Offensively, the Bulldogs employed a deep rotation of fullbacks, blocking backs, halfbacks and wingbacks for most of their points. The best of the bunch was Lou Smyth, whose nickname was "Hammer." At 6-1 and 200 pounds, Smyth led the fledgling league in both passing touchdowns

Among the play options of player/coach Guy Chamberlin (below) was the tackle-eligible pass, which he used with Henry and Lyman.

(six) and rushing touchdowns (seven).

Ben Jones (six rushing TDs), Cecil B. "Tex" Grigg (three rushing TDs, one passing TD and one receiving TD), Doc Elliott (six rushing TDs) and Harry Robb (one rushing TD) also contributed enough to be named All-Pros on at least one of the three lists published at the end of the season.

One of the ends, Elmer Ellsworth "Bird" Carroll, accounted for two receiving touchdowns. Chamberlin, who also played end, caught a pair of TD passes, too.

As the season developed for the Bulldogs, they were challenged only a few times. The one game they didn't win happened midway through the year when they tied the All-Americans, 3-3, at Buffalo. That game followed a pair of narrow 7-3 victories at home against Akron and on the road against Paddy Driscoll's Chicago Cardinals.

Perhaps the season's most meaningful victory was an October 21 game against George Halas' Chicago Bears at what was then known as Cub Park, now Wrigley Field. Chamberlin had been hired away from the Bears before the 1922 season. Canton won, 6-0.

The 1923 season was the last hurrah for the mighty Canton Bulldogs. Team owner Ralph Hay decided the club needed a larger venue than Lakeside Park, the tiny minor league baseball stadium it called home. Before the next season opened, he sold the team to Sammy Deutsch, who owned the NFL's Cleveland Indians. Deutsch merged the two teams in Cleveland, and won the NFL championship in 1924.

Canton was home to another pro team called the Bulldogs several years later, and actually lured Thorpe back to play again in 1926. But that version never measured up the glory days of 1922-23.

Henry and Lyman led a defensive unit that held 1923 opponents to 19 points and one touchdown.

24

Would he, or wouldn't he? Should he, or shouldn't he? The debate raged in Denver and around the National Football League in the spring and summer of 1998. Would John Elway retire? Should John Elway retire? After three unsuccessful tries at the Super Bowl in the '80s, he had finally taken the Broncos to an NFL championship at the end of the 1997 season. Denver upset Green Bay, 31-24, in Super Bowl XXXII. Wasn't that enough? Shouldn't Elway, who played his 15th season in '97, go out that way? A winner in the biggest game of all?

It took him well into the summer to announce his decision to come back for another year. When he did, Broncos fans could finally exhale. They'd have "The Franchise" around for at least one more season.

One more very memorable season, as it developed. Elway and the Broncos were unstoppable on offense. They scored 501 points, an average of 31.3 per game and the sixth-highest point total in league history. They averaged 381 yards of total offense. And they won their first 13 games, threatening into mid-December to match the Miami Dolphins' unbeaten

Trigger man John Elway (7) returned for a 1998 swan song that sounded sweet to Broncos fans.

and untied season of 1972. After the seventh game of the year, an easy victory over a good Jacksonville team, the watch was on. Would Denver ever lose?

By December 13, when they finally did lose, the Broncos had won 18 straight games dating back to 1997 and including the postseason. That tied an NFL record.

There were a couple of similarities between the '72 Dolphins and the '98 Broncos that went beyond the winning streaks. The Dolphins reached perfection in 1972 playing most of the year with 38-year-old backup quarterback Earl Morrall, who replaced Bob Griese after an injury in

> **Tailback Terrell Davis rushed for 2,008 yards and 21 touchdowns.**

the fifth game. Elway missed all or parts of four games in the '98 season with bruised ribs and a pulled hamstring. For a month, Broncomaniacs held their breath as 36-year-old Bubby Brister took the snaps. Brister, and the Broncos, kept winning.

A second similarity was imposing running games that took the pressure off those backup quarterbacks. Miami's perfect record came on the strength of a power attack led by Larry Csonka, Mercury Morris and Jim Kiick. Denver's offense was run-powered, too, by tailback Terrell Davis, who became only the fourth running back in NFL history to rush for more than 2,000 yards. Davis finished with 2,008 yards and 21 rushing touchdowns, also a league-best mark.

Davis' presence and the strength of Denver's running game help explain Elway's decision to play one more year. It took the Broncos most of his career to achieve it, but by the late '90s the team had finally reached an offensive balance that did not require Elway to be a one-man band. If anything, Davis' dominance made Elway more effective. Defenses had to try to stop Davis first, which opened up passing lanes Elway rarely saw even during Denver's Super Bowl seasons in the 1980s.

Because he missed almost four complete games, Elway's passing totals don't measure up to his best statistical years. But he threw for 2,806 yards and 22 touchdowns against only 10 interceptions. Not bad for 12-plus games.

Very few of those 22 touchdown passes needed to be the come-from-behind variety that characterized Elway's earlier greatness. The Broncos of 1998 jumped on top so early and so often that the offense spent most fourth quarters protecting leads rather than forging them. In their first six games, they outscored opponents 87-7 in the first quarter and 135-50 in the first half.

The early leads protected a Denver defense that was good, but not great. Very few teams were able to stay for long with the game plans they'd designed to take advantage of the Broncos' perceived defensive shortcomings. Opponent after opponent had to ditch ball control in favor of desperate comeback attempts.

Denver beat Dallas, 42-23, with an early onslaught in the second week. Davis gained 191 yards on 23 carries, and scored on touchdown runs of 63, 59 and 3 yards. On October 4, Philadelphia was dispatched, 41-16, with a comparable early explosion. In those first six weeks, the Broncos only trailed a team on one occasion, when Oakland took a 10-7 lead in the second quarter on September 20. Five minutes later, that deficit was history. Denver roared back to a 34-17 win.

Against the Jaguars in the seventh game, Jason Elam tied a 28-year-old NFL record by kicking a 63-yard field goal in Denver's 37-24 victory. It seemed there was nothing the Broncos' offense couldn't do. On December 6, they won their 13th straight, 35-31, over

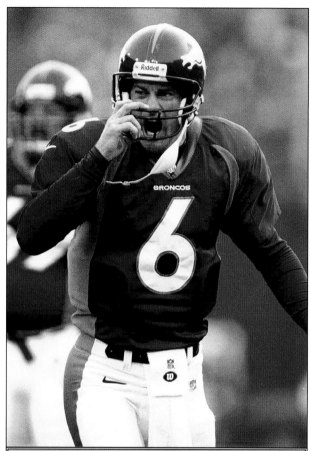

Backup QB Bubby Brister (6) and receiver Ed McCaffrey (87) made big contributions in a 14-2 regular season.

Kansas City. It was the 10th time in 13 games they had scored at least 30 points. The fewest they had managed was 21, in a 21-16 win over Seattle.

Two weeks after the Chiefs' game, Denver was scheduled to play a December 21 game against the Dolphins on Monday Night Football in Miami. Only a game against the 5-8 New York Giants stood between the

ahead, 20-16. There would be no perfect season.

The next week, the Broncos came out flat in Florida against a Dolphins defense that gave up the fewest points in the league. Elway was only 13-of-36 for 151 yards and two interceptions. Davis gained just 29 yards on 16 carries and Denver lost, 31-21, for the second straight week.

The Broncos already had clinched home-field

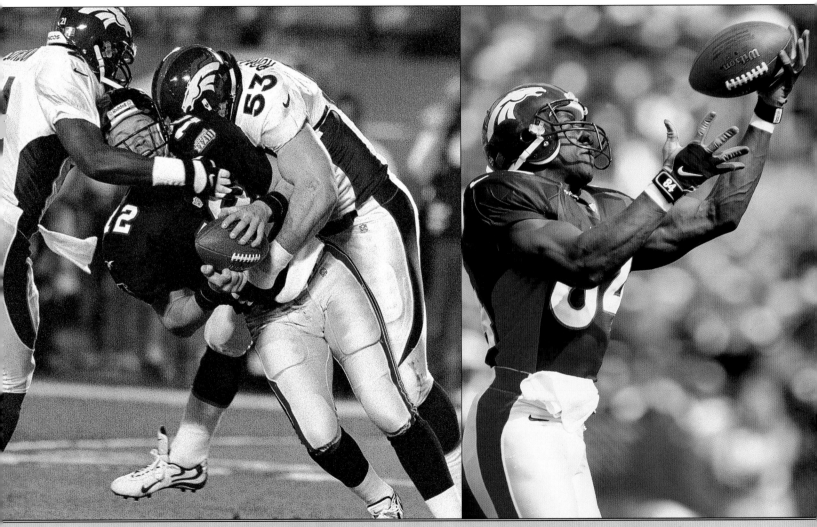

Linebacker Bill Romanowski (53) was an imposing defender; tight end Shannon Sharpe was a big-play receiver.

Broncos and a showdown with the franchise that boasted the league's only perfect record.

But a funny thing happened on the way to Miami. With 48 seconds to play in Giants Stadium, New York quarterback Kent Graham completed a 37-yard touchdown pass to wide receiver Amani Toomer that put the Giants

advantage throughout the AFC playoffs, but they only had one regular-season game left to regain the momentum of their first 13 weeks. Against Seattle, they found it. Elway passed for 338 yards and four touchdowns, one of which made him only the third quarterback in the history of the league with 300 or more career TD passes. Davis, who needed 170 yards on the ground to reach 2,000 for the year and was playing the Seahawks game with a sore back, gained 54 in the first quarter, 28 in the second period, 51 in the third.

On a 15-yard run in the fourth quarter, he made it. He finished the game with 178 yards. On the strength of 511 yards of total offense, the Broncos beat the Seahawks, 28-21, and righted themselves in time for the playoffs.

Their first-round opponent was Miami, just three weeks after the Dolphins had humbled them. Davis, held to 29 yards in Miami, exploded for 199. Denver 38, Miami 3.

The Jets, the opponent in the AFC

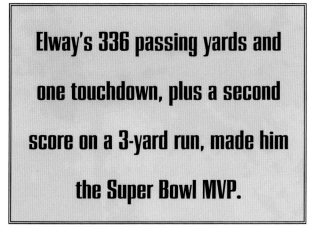

Elway's 336 passing yards and one touchdown, plus a second score on a 3-yard run, made him the Super Bowl MVP.

Championship Game, had allowed only two running backs to gain more than 100 yards all season. Davis gained 167 and the Broncos won, 23-10, to earn the right to defend their Super Bowl title against Atlanta and Dan Reeves, who had coached Denver for 12 seasons.

After the 34-19 victory over the Falcons, it became clear why Elway had returned for that one final season in 1998. The peak he reached in Super Bowl XXXIII was higher even than the one he and the team had climbed against the Packers the year before. Elway's 336 passing yards and one touchdown, plus a second score on a 3-yard run, made him the Super Bowl MVP.

It was his last game. You can't go out any better than that.

Johnny Unitas passed for 95 yards. That's Johnny U., the ultimate competitor, toughest quarterback to ever play the game. Unitas, in his prime. For three hours on a chilly, blustery, December afternoon at Cleveland's Municipal Stadium, the great Unitas tried everything, called on everything he knew and everything he had. And he had plenty. He had Raymond Berry. John Mackey. Jimmy Orr. Lenny Moore. Jim Parker. He had Don Shula as his coach.

And what did all that talent, all that experience, do for him? A piddling 95 yards and no touchdowns.

That's how good Cleveland's defense was that day.

The Browns were good enough to shut out one of the best offenses the NFL has produced. Their 27-0 victory over Unitas' Baltimore Colts in the 1964 NFL Championship Game transformed Cleveland from a very solid, very strong team into one of the most memorable clubs in NFL history.

At the time, Cleveland's title-game victory was considered an upset. The Baltimore team the Browns beat was, in the opinion of most of the day's observers, supposed to be better. The Colts came into the championship game with the No. 1 offense in the league, led by five future Hall of Fame players. And they didn't score a point.

Quarterback Frank Ryan (13) did the math and Cleveland rolled over Baltimore in a one-sided title game.

1964 Cleveland Browns

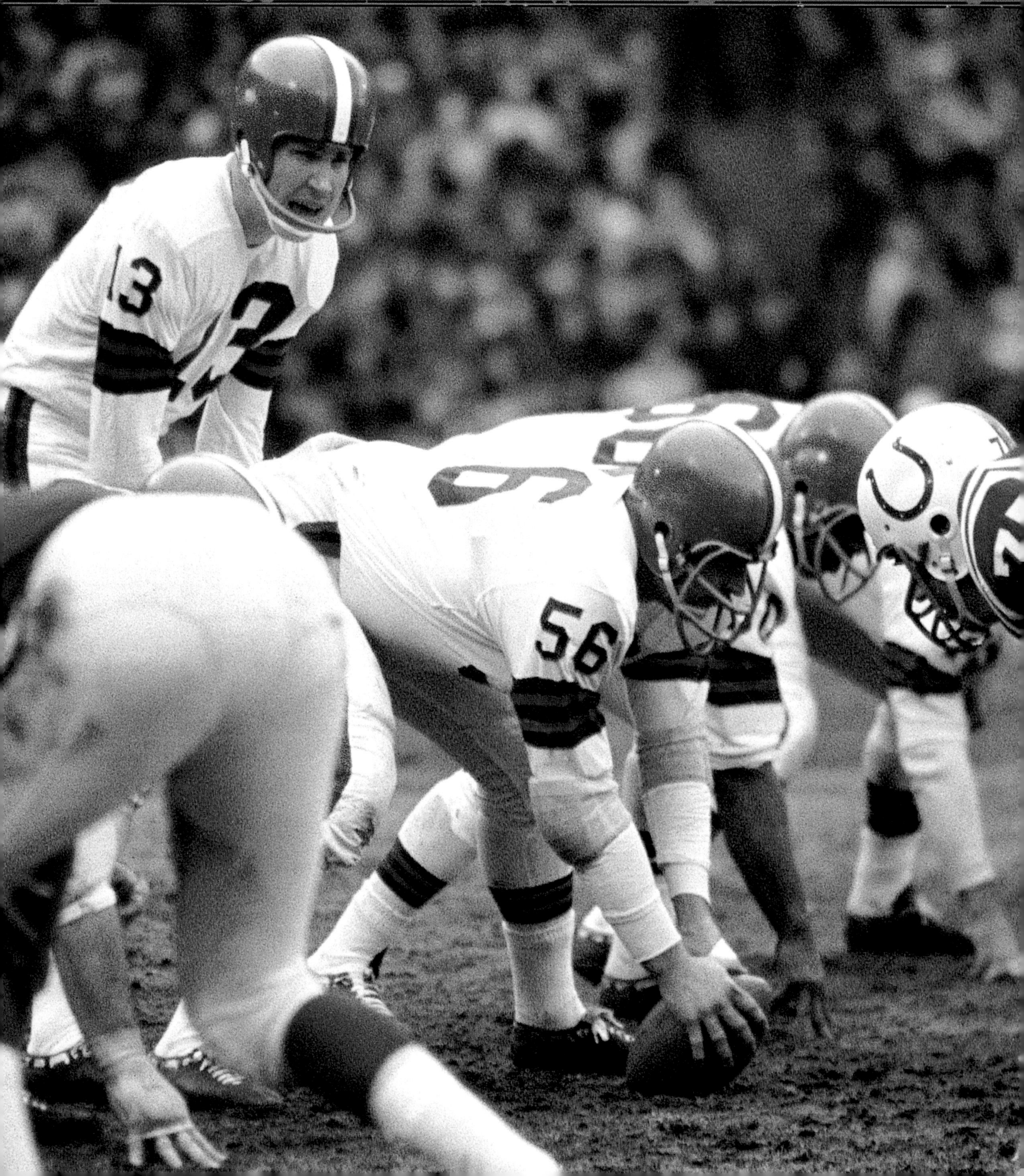

Now, in retrospect, it's difficult to think of a unit that featured Jim Brown, Paul Warfield, Lou Groza, Gary Collins and Frank Ryan as an underdog to anybody. But sometimes the measure of a team needs to factor in the caliber of its opponents. In 1964, the Browns needed Baltimore and that 27-0 victory for their place in history.

They compiled a 10-3-1 record during the regular season, which was good enough to win the Eastern Conference championship but not good enough to clinch it until the season's last day. The Browns stumbled in their next-to-last game, falling to St. Louis, 28-19. A loss to the Giants in the final week would have sent the Cardinals into the championship game.

Against the Giants, Ryan threw only 13 passes. But he completed 12 of them for 202

Second-year tackle Jim Kanicki (69 above) was capable of shutting down the middle, and third-year receiver Gary Collins (86 below) was a talented game-breaker, as the Colts discovered the hard way.

yards and five touchdowns. For good measure, he also ran 13 yards for a sixth TD.

Ryan, who brought an IQ of 155 to the reading of defenses, was obviously a thinking-man's quarterback. As he led the Browns through the regular season and to the NFL championship that season, he also finished up his work on a Ph.D. in mathematics from Rice University, titling his dissertation, "A Characterization of Asymptotic Values of a Function Holomorphic in the Unit Disc."

A month after the season ended, Dr. Ryan was teaching math at Rice.

With Brown leading the league in rushing (1,446 yards) and Ryan throwing to the rookie Warfield (52 catches, 920 yards and 9 touchdowns) and the third-year veteran Collins (35 receptions for 544 yards and 8 TDs) at the two wide receiver spots, those math skills came in handy tallying up the Browns' scores. They finished behind only Baltimore in points that year.

The line was solid, featuring Monte Clark, Dick Schafrath, John Wooten, Gene Hickerson and John Morrow. Under second-year head coach Blanton Collier, those five perfected an option-blocking scheme that gave them freedom to move defensive players wherever they could so that Brown could use his outstanding vision and heads-up running style to slash through whatever hole they opened.

But the defense hadn't dominated, at least not leading up to the title game. In 10 of the Browns' 14 regular-season games, including the last six, the opponent scored 20 points or more. The Browns appeared to be vulnerable to a passing attack, and looked especially at risk against a passing attack as polished and efficient as the one Unitas brought to Cleveland on December 27. Johnny U. threw for 2,824 yards that season, with only six interceptions and 19 touchdowns.

The appearance that the Browns might be defenseless against Unitas and his trio of receivers (Berry and Orr at wideouts, Mackey at tight end) was deceiving. Many of the yards the Browns gave up to the pass during the regular season came late in games as they protected leads given them by the offense. Teams racked up yardage and occasional points with short passes underneath a prevent defense.

The Browns could be bent, but they were rarely broken when it mattered.

Against the Colts, it mattered. Against the Colts, Cleveland cornerbacks Bernie Parrish and Walter Beach cut off the short slant routes and quick out patterns that Berry, Orr and Mackey ran so well. Against the Colts, the Browns' interior defensive linemen kept constant pressure on Unitas, recording six sacks and forcing two interceptions.

Defensive tackle Jim Kanicki, in particular, starred. Kanicki had three of the sacks, a remarkable performance in light of his

Cornerback Bernie Parrish (30) and partners in the secondary knew how to handle receivers—and they proved it against Baltimore.

one-on-one matchups with Parker, Baltimore's future Hall of Fame offensive tackle.

By halftime, the Colts were stunned and confused, not to mention scoreless. Their high-powered offense had managed only 127 net yards.

But Cleveland, playing conservatively on offense, hadn't scored, either. With two quarters to play, the score was 0-0.

Then Cleveland's famous winter weather interceded. Early in the third period, Colts punter Tom Gilburg tried to kick straight into the gale whipping off Lake Erie, and watched the ball blow straight back toward him. His short punt set Groza up for a 42-yard field goal and a 3-0 Browns lead.

On Cleveland's next possession, Brown, who finished with 114 yards, broke free on a 46-yard gain; and Ryan, with the wind, passed to the 6-foot-4 Collins over 5-11 Baltimore cornerback Bobby Boyd for an 18-yard touchdown. When Ryan hit Collins again for another score, this one on a wind-aided bomb from 42 yards out later in the third quarter, Cleveland led 17-0.

Another Groza field goal and a third Ryan-to-Collins TD pass in the fourth quarter wrapped up the scoring.

The Colts' offense, meanwhile, never made the right adjustments. In 22 second-half plays, Baltimore gained only 54 yards. Unitas finished with those 95 meaningless passing yards.

By contrast, Ryan stayed on the roll he'd started the week before against the Giants. The Colts had allowed the fewest points in the league during the regular season, but Ryan riddled

The Browns' offense revolved around annual rushing champion Jim Brown.

Baltimore's defense for 206 yards on 11 completions in 18 attempts and the three TD passes to Collins.

As a footnote to his performance, the math professor may have been a bit too calculating in the closing seconds of the Colts' game that day. With 26 seconds left, the fans stormed the field and began to tear down the goalposts. Cleveland was up 27-0 and had the ball at the Baltimore 16-yard line.

The officials suggested the game be declared

Ryan had the option of throwing to Paul Warfield (above 42) ...

over, but Ryan insisted on playing out the clock. He lost the debate. The game ended. Still, at least one Baltimore player apparently felt Ryan was trying to run up the score, and carried a grudge into the Pro Bowl two weeks later. Colts defensive end Gino Marchetti claimed before the Pro Bowl that he wanted another shot at the Browns' quarterback, and he got it in the all-star game's third quarter. Marchetti knocked Ryan out of action with a dislocated shoulder.

... or handing the ball off to Brown (below). The multi-dimensional offense left defenses guessing all season.

1934 CHICAGO BEARS

But for the weather, the 1934 Chicago Bears might have been the first NFL team to be undefeated and untied through the regular season and playoffs. Chicago stormed to a 13-0 record in '34, outscoring its opponents 286-86. The Bears were a heavy favorite to defeat the 8-5 New York Giants in the league championship game on December 9. But in the second half on a frozen field at the Polo Grounds, the Giants put on basketball sneakers rushed over from nearby Manhattan College and zipped to four fourth-quarter touchdowns and a 30-13 victory over the stunned Bears.

Until then, Chicago had been unstoppable. Rookie Beattie Feathers of Tennessee led the league in touchdowns with nine and became the first professional player to rush for more than 1,000 yards. He finished with 1,004. Fullback Bronko Nagurski, who did much of the blocking for Feathers, gained 586 yards and scored seven touchdowns. The team also featured end Bill Hewitt, guard Joe Kopcha, tackle Link Lyman, center Eddie Kawal and reserve back Red Grange in his last season.

In 1934, Bronko Nagurski rushed for 586 yards and was lead blocker for the NFL's first 1,000-yard rusher.

QBs Earl Morrall (left), Johnny Unitas and Bobby Layne (below) played big roles in their teams' success.

1968 BALTIMORE COLTS

They were the "other" team in Super Bowl III, in which Joe Namath guaranteed, and delivered, a Jets victory. Over the years, the shock of that upset has obscured the dominance with which the Baltimore Colts rolled through the 1968 NFL season.

They were 13-1 during the regular season, outscoring their opponents by an average margin of more than 18 points. Their only loss was to Cleveland on October 20 by a 30-20 score, and the Colts avenged that defeat with a 34-0 shellacking of the Browns in the NFL Championship Game. Led by linemen Bubba Smith and Billy Ray Smith Sr., and defensive back Bobby Boyd, the Colts' defense recorded four shutouts and gave up the fewest points in either league.

After Johnny Unitas had injured his elbow, backup Earl Morrall played quarterback for most of the year. Morrall passed for 2,909 yards and 26 touchdowns, and was named the NFL's most valuable player. Tom Matte, who gained 116 rushing yards in the Super Bowl, led the way on the ground; tight end John Mackey (45 catches for 644 yards and five TDs) was the leading receiver.

1953 DETROIT LIONS

The indefatigable Bobby Layne had 4:10 to save Detroit's 1953 season on December 27 in Briggs Stadium, and he was short one of his starting wide receivers. No sweat. That was 2:08 more than he needed.

Down 16-10 to Cleveland in the NFL Championship Game, the Lions took over on their own 20-yard line. Layne passed 17 yards to right end Jim Doran, who was in the game only because starter Leon Hart had been injured earlier. Several plays later, Layne eschewed a screen pass called by Detroit coach Buddy Parker and threw deep from the 33-yard line instead. Doran, a step behind Cleveland's Warren Lahr, caught it at the 10 and scored with 2:08 still to play. Doak Walker's extra-point kick made the Lions 17-16 winners.

Detroit was 10-2 in winning the Western Conference. In the Championship Game, the Lions forced Browns quarterback Otto Graham into his worst day as a pro. He completed just 2-of-15 passes for 20 yards.

Layne led the way for the '53 Lions, throwing for 2,088 yards and 16 touchdowns. Jack Christiansen topped the league in interceptions with 12.

Photo Credits

R=Right L=Left T=Top B=Bottom M=Middle

Cover Photo: First Row: Dilip Vishwanat, Second Row: TSN Archives, Third Row: Malcolm Emmons, Fourth Row: Malcolm Emmons
Back Cover: Malcolm Emmons

Contributing Photographers:
AP/Wide World Photos: 83, 84, 85T, 85B, 86B, 87T, 92T, 93, 113, 114, 115T, 115B, 116, 117L, 117R, 125, 126T, 127, 128B, 137, 138.
Bettmann/CORBIS: 53.
Vernon Biever: 11, 12B, 23, 24T, 26B, 27, 80, 81B, 89.
Cleveland Browns Archive: 54, 55T.
Cleveland Press Collection of Cleveland State University: 57.
Jonathan Daniel/Allsport: 145T.
Louis DeLuca: 108, 109L, 109R, 110T, 110B, 111R.
Albert Dickson/The Sporting News: 6, 133T, 161, 162, 163T, 165.
Tony Duffy/Allsport: 67B, 68.
Malcolm Emmons: 4, 7, 12T, 13T, 13B, 14T, 14B, 15, 16, 17, 18, 19T. 19B, 21, 22, 24B, 25, 29, 30, 31, 32T, 32B, 33, 34T, 34B, 35, 37, 40, 42, 59, 60, 61T, 61B, 62, 63, 65, 66, 67T, 69, 71, 72T, 72B, 73, 74, 75T, 75B, 77, 78, 79, 81T, 90, 102, 103T, 103B, 104T, 104B, 105, 119, 120, 121T, 121B, 122T, 122B, 123, 149, 150B, 151T, 151B, 152T, 152B, 167, 168T, 168B, 169, 170, 171T, 171B, 173T, 176.
Otto Greule Jr./Allsport: 46.
Hall of Fame/NFL Photos: 155, 156, 157, 158, 159.
Bob Leverone/The Sporting News: 133B, 135.
Lew Portnoy: 8-9, 39, 43, 101.
Earl Richardson/Allsport: 145B.
Robert Seale/The Sporting News: 164L.
Rick Stewart/Allsport: 50T, 50B, 98T, 99.
Stiller-Lefebvre Collection: 126B, 128T, 129, 139, 140T, 140B, 141T, 141B.
The Sporting News Archives: 2T, 2B, 26T, 38T, 38B, 41T, 41B, 45, 47L, 47R, 48, 49, 51L, 51R, 55B, 91, 92B, 95, 96, 97, 98B, 107, 143, 144, 146T, 146B, 147, 148, 150T, 153, 163B, 164R, 172, 173B.
Dilip Vishwanat/The Sporting News: 131, 132, 134L, 134R, 174-175.